The year 2010 marks the 175th anniversary of the Great Western Railway. This publication pays homage to Charles Benjamin Collett who was certainly the GWR's most prolific Chief Mechanical Engineer. Collett presided over the introduction of 15 new locomotive classes and eight rebuilds or additions to other designs, an incredible combined total of some 2589 steam locomotives.

Collett served the GWR from 1893 until 1941, and having joined the company as a junior draughtsman steadily advanced through the ranks to become deputy CME to the great CJ Churchward in 1919. Upon Churchward's retirement the GWR board appointed Collett to the post of CME in 1922, a post he held for 19 years. At the time of his appointment the company had a locomotive shortage in general and in particular an urgent need for fast reliable modern express passenger locomotives.

Addressing the problem Collett took the earlier Churchward Star class design as the basis for his new four-cylinder 4-6-0 design, and thus the Castle class was born. Right from the delivery of the first locomotives the GWR realised that enlarged Star or not, in the Castle design they had a real winner. By the time British Railways dropped the last Castle and King fires the Collett four-cylinder designs had earned the respect of thousands of railwaymen and millions of rail travellers, over the best part of five decades.

As the Castle was an accepted development of the Star class then it was not surprising that the Collett King class engines, introduced in 1927 were at first seen as enlarged Castle class engines. But by incorporating new design features and in part moving away from standard GWR engineering principles of the time Collett produced yet another winner. Indeed the unique King class was claimed by many knowledgeable commentators to be the best British express locomotive of its day, and some even claimed the engines to be the finest 4-6-0 locomotives to ever run on the UK railway network! However the one question always asked is why only 30 Kings were produced, when after all 171 Castles were built?

Thanks to the UK rail preservation movement in conjunction with private locomotive owners and organisations like the Great Western Society, the charismatic Castle and exquisite King class designs can still be admired, with thankfully examples often to be seen in steam and even hauling trains on the national railway network. There are eight Castle class and three King class locomotives in preservation.

This British Steam GWR 175 special edition contains all the relevant facts and figures appertaining to Collett's four-cylinder 4-6-0 Castle and King class locomotives. In addition there are over 130 photographic images, the majority of which are published for the first time. **British Steam – Castles & Kings** was written compiled and edited in the spring of 2010. **Keith Langston**

Preserved Castle class 4-6-0 No 5043 EARL OF MOUNT EDGCUMBE is pictured at speed passing Hatton North Junction on the return trip to Birmingham (18 April 2010) following an earlier 'Bristolian' weekend. *Phil Neale*

∎INTRODUCTION

The Great Western Railway always saw itself as an industry leader, and as such was an unashamedly publicity-seeking organisation. Historians have rightly commented that the organisation was in fact the most charismatic railway company always striving to provide its customers with the very best in comfort and punctuality, while doing so with panache and style. Indeed the GWR's locomotive fleet was noted for its striking distinctive liveries, embracing a generous, but nevertheless tasteful use of copper embellishments.

The Castle and King class four-cylinder 4-6-0 locomotives designed by the company's Chief Mechanical Engineer (1922-1941) Charles Benjamin Collett were not only the epitome of grace and style but also express passenger locomotives of the very highest calibre. Right from the start the new engines attracted comment and publicity, firstly the Castle class was introduced by the GWR publicity department as being 'Britain's Most Powerful Express Passenger Locomotive'. When the first of the class was exhibited in London it was met with almost universal approval and soon went on to prove itself worthy of the aforementioned title when trialled against similar sized locomotives manufactured by other railway companies.

The detractors were quick to point out that Collett's Castle class locomotives were simply a development of his predecessor GJ Churchward's Star class engines. However simply making a bigger version of something is no iron clad guarantee of success and due credit must be given to Collett for making 'his' new design 'work'. It should be noted that the success of the class was also in no small way attributable to groundbreaking new production techniques which Collett introduced at Swindon Works.

The class was produced between August 1923 and July 1946 by the GWR, and then between May 1948 and August 1950 by British Railways with all 171 of the class being rebuilt/built at Swindon Works. As the Castle class engines were tagged enlarged Star locomotives it therefore came as no surprise that the 1927 introduction by Collett of his King class attracted the comment that those machines were not new at all but actually only Super Castles! The King class engines regained for the GWR the title of 'Britain's Most Powerful Express Passenger Locomotive' which the Castle class had earlier lost to the Southern Railway Lord Nelson class.

The first King locomotive left Swindon Works in June 1927 and the last of the 30-strong class was outshopped in August 1930. Both classes of engines were modified to good effect during their working lifetimes with the change to varying specifications of superheated boiler having the most beneficial effect on performance. The GWR and then BR/WR put both Castle and King class locomotives to good use and the types became loved and respected by railwaymen and enthusiasts alike.

Recall if you will a famous TV advertisement in which an American gentleman tells us that he was so impressed with the performance of a certain brand of electric razor that he 'bought the company'.

In 1926 the largest of the big four railway companies, the London Midland & Scottish, tried unsuccessfully to buy 50 Castle four-cylinder 4-6-0 locomotives from the GWR. Unable to buy the Castles or indeed the company in 1932 the LMSR did the next best thing, they successfully 'bought' the services of one William A Stanier!

He reportedly arrived at Crewe with a wooden chest full of Swindon inspired drawings! Stanier was Collett's Principal Assistant from 1922 to 1932.

For the record the American entrepreneur was Victor Kiam, the razor was a Remington.

Under reconstruction and due to steam again in 2010, ex GWR King class 4-6-0 No 6023 KING EDWARD II is pictured at its Didcot base in April 2010.

Phil Neale

THE COLLETT LEGACY

In 1948 British Railways inherited some 2288 locomotives which could be directly attributed to Charles Benjamin Collett OBE, representing almost 60 per cent of the ex GWR total. Collett served the Great Western Railway for the majority of his working life finally becoming Chief Mechanical Engineer (CME) of that organisation in 1922, a position which he held until his retirement in 1941. Prominent among his locomotives were the powerful four-cylinder 4-6-0 Castle and King classes, but those fine engines were by no means his only successful locomotives.

Collett GWR King No 6027 KING RICHARD I is pictured in pristine condition at Didcot during May 1961. The locomotive had just completed a visit to Swindon Works and it can be seen that at this time no shed code plate was carried. *David Anderson*

Loco No 6027 entered service in July 1930 and was first allocated to Old Oak Common. BR shed allocations included Newton Abbot (83A), Plymouth Laira (83D) and Wolverhampton Stafford Road (84A) from where the locomotive was withdrawn.

CHURCHWARD'S HEIR APPARENT

It is a generally held belief that Collett was an 'improver' of designs attributed to his predecessor George Jackson Churchward. Indeed many considered Collett's predecessor to be the greatest of all the GWR locomotive designers. Perhaps in the full sense of the word Collett was not strictly speaking a locomotive designer, but he was undoubtedly an accomplished engineer, administrator and also respected for his organisational abilities.

The son of a journalist Collett was born at Paddington, London, in 1871 and his formal education was at the Merchant Taylors' School, London and the City and Guilds College. Leaving university he went to work as an engineering pupil for Maudsley, Son & Field Ltd of Lambeth, an established company of marine engine builders. In 1893 at 22 years of age Collett entered the hallowed portals of Swindon Works for the first time.

Noted for being a diligent and methodical worker he served as a junior

draughtsman until in 1898 he was appointed to the position of Assistant to the Chief Draughtsman. Collett's first senior position was that of Technical Inspector, Swindon Works, a post he held for just over a year. Appointed to the post of Assistant Works Manager, Swindon, in 1901 Collett's not inconsiderable engineering abilities cannot have failed to come to the attention of one GJ Churchward who was at that time Chief Assistant to the then GWR Locomotive Superintendent William Dean.

Collett served in senior positions under two GWR CMEs, Dean and Churchward; he would have greatly profited from the experience he gained during his 20 years under Churchward who was GWR Locomotive Superintendent (1902-1916) and then Chief Mechanical Engineer (1916-1921). In 1912 Collett was appointed to the post of Works Manager, Swindon. As his career progressed it became obvious to many that Collett was effectively Churchward's heir apparent.

COLLEAGUES

It is interesting to note that among his colleagues during progress through the GWR engineering ranks was another young engineer, one William A Stanier, later of LMS fame. Stanier joined the GWR as an apprentice in 1892 and in 1906 (during Collett's spell as Assistant Works Manager, Swindon) Stanier became Assistant to the Works Manager, Swindon. In 1912 Stanier became Assistant Works Manager, Swindon as Collett became Works Manager, Swindon.

Stanier's career continued to track that of Collett and in 1922 when the latter was appointed Great Western Railway Chief Mechanical Engineer Stanier became Principal Assistant to the CME. Stanier, when aged 56, left the GWR for pastures new in 1932 after he had deduced that the clearly signalled continuance 'in post' of Collett (then aged 61) was blocking his upward move to the CME's office. History proved Stanier to be correct as Collett continued in the job for a further nine years. Collett and Stanier were both very certainly influenced by the work of Churchward and, of course the experience they gained from working in the CME's design team at Swindon.

During his formative years Collett did not in the main spend time around running sheds and on locomotive footplates he was instead very much a 'works' man, thus the greater part of his later to flourish expertise lay in developing engineering practices and improving work flow methods. Before becoming CME he had spent over 20 years working to improve boiler manufacturing to great effect and additionally rationalising rolling stock and improving locomotive repair facilities.

Great Western folklore would have it that Churchward and Collett were not necessarily the best of friends, but solid proof of that commonly held belief is hard to find. However what is certain is the fact that they were personality wise very different people, indeed 'chalk and cheese' would not be a misplaced appraisal of the diverse personae of the two engineers. The two men did without doubt make a formidable team furthermore Churchward's standard locomotive designs suited the GWR and accordingly Collett was the perfect choice of engineer to bring into being the new and improved production methods needed in order to construct 20th century steam locomotives.

Above: **Delivering the milk! Churchward Star 4-6-0 N0 4062 MALMESBURY ABBEY on the Up stopper with passenger stock and milk tanks near Thingley Junction, a fasinating image from 1956. No 4062 entered service for the GWR in May 1922 and was scrapped by British Railways in November 1956.** *Colour-Rail/PM Alexander*

Opposite: **GWR Churchward Star 4000 class 4-6-0 No 4061 GLASTONBURY ABBEY pictured inside Old Oak Common shed (81A) in September 1955. Built at Swindon in 1922 No 4061 was withdrawn by BR in March 1957.** *Colour-Rail/TB Owen*

COLLETT – GWR CHIEF MECHANICAL ENGINEER

Churchward was a hard act to follow as he was reportedly an outgoing man with great charisma who ruled with a very firm hand, indeed the word domineering has even been used to describe some aspects of his management style. By comparison Collett was perhaps a milder man and almost certainly less domineering than his predecessor but he was also a hard task master, who insisted upon top quality work from his staff and demanded their absolute loyalty. However Collett did gain the reputation of being a very fair man and that aspect of his personality did indeed earn him the respect of colleagues. Collett did not seek to attract friends and his apparent standoffish manner meant that other members of the management team did not on a personal level seek to closely associate themselves with him.

Preserved GWR Collett Castle '4073' class 4-6-0 No 4079 PENDENNIS CASTLE is pictured at Oxford in May 1961. *David Anderson*

GWR Collett Castle No 5054 EARL OF DUCIE at Reading with an Up South Wales express, April 1947. This loco entered service with the name LAMPHEY CASTLE and was subsequently renamed in September 1937. *Colour-Rail/NH James*

Castle No 5054 was built 1936 and first allocated to Old Oak Common depot. Under BR other shed allocations included Cardiff Canton (86C) Bristol Bath Road (82A) and Gloucester Horton Road (85B) from where the engine was withdrawn.

Soon after his appointment to the post of CME Collett got to work modernising the former Rhymney Railway Caerphilly works which he comprehensively reorganised and equipped to become the maintenance and repair centre for GWR locomotives and rolling stock allocated to the Welsh valleys. Some five years later the workshops at Wolverhampton Stafford Road were exhaustively upgraded under Collett's supervision in order to maintain all GWR locomotives in the northern area.

Much to the delight of the GWR board of directors the reorganisation of workshops and procedures instigated by Collett led to sizeable reductions in manufacturing costs. Of great importance was the development of techniques associated with the optical alignment of locomotive frames, cylinders and motion using equipment supplied by the famous Zeiss Company. Swindon claimed that employing such meticulous practices turned steam locomotives into precision machines. Improved performances validated that claim. Collett also continued the expansion of the GWR Automatic Train Control system which during his time was installed on almost all of the company's important routes.

ROLLING STOCK

Collett was associated with other GWR landmark decisions not least of which was the introduction of the Laycock buckeye coupler, a move which greatly benefited the company. He also worked at improving coaching stock and while his 1925 articulated suburban stock may have invited a degree of criticism other innovations and improvements were judged to be highly successful, notably his 1931 Super Saloons and 1935 Centenary coaches. We should also remember that Collett reintroduced the popular chocolate and cream livery for coaching stock early on in his period in office.

Starting with the premise that good bogie design is paramount to the 'ride quality' of a passenger coach Collett carried out novel tests using a seven-coach consist which became known as the 'Whitewash Train'. In short each coach incorporated differently designed bogies, and in each vehicle the toilet flush box was filled with different coloured shades of whitewash. Observers, if that is the word, were posted in each WC cubicle and instructed to release wash whenever a bad 'lurch' was experienced.

Thereafter the resultant rainbow of colours observed on the ballast would indicate which bogie reacted to a particular track defect etc. Of course if all the colours had been released at one point then perchance the track was itself in need of repair. The concept of the 'Whitewash Train' was a far cry from the precision of the Zeiss Optical frame alignment system! But reportedly it was nevertheless effective.

Above: **A great locomotive portrait (possibly taken at Hereford with the Nelson Monument at Castle Green in the distance?) the engine at this time is carrying a Hereford (85C) shedplate. This 1959 study of King No 6018 KING HENRY VI shows clearly the classic King look (double chimney). Note the out-of-use route indicator frame resting on the step of the bufferbeam.** *Colour-Rail*

Built in 1938 King No 6018 was first allocated to Plymouth Laira. Under BR other allocations included Old Oak Common (81A) and Cardiff Canton (88A formerly 86C) from where the locomotive was withdrawn. KING HENRY VI was later reinstated to work the last King journey under BR WR.

Preserved Dukedog '9xxx' class 4-4-0 No 9017 is pictured during the 2009 Steel, Steam & Stars event at Llangollen Railway. By combining parts of the extremely old Duke and Bulldog classes Collett formed the 'Earl' class, engines which became known as Dukedogs. *Author*

A PRIVATE MAN

Tragedy struck in Collett's personal life when in 1923 Ethelwyn May (a vicar's daughter) and his wife of 10 years' standing became seriously ill and unexpectedly died. His wife's untimely death engendered in him an interest in esoteric medicine and a linked belief in the value of dietary remedies. Indeed by employing such methods he claimed to have overcome a cancer-related illness of his own not long after her death. Always a private man, thereafter Collett became even more so, and rarely if ever attended works social functions.

Collett received an OBE in 1919 in recognition of his work in the production of munitions during the First World War. There were reportedly many instances of serious friction between Collett and officials

of the Ministry of Labour during that period and the whole episode had a marked effect on his future attitude to government officialdom. So much so that when at the onset of World War Two the GWR were again asked to make available production facilities for the manufacture of munitions Collett was reluctant to allow the workshops to undertake such work.

His objections were noted by the Paddington board members but overruled. Consequently he asked the GWR board to take note of his concerns as he feared that locomotives and rolling stock would fall into disrepair due to a resultant lack of facilities and materials. Anyone au fait with the appalling state of the railways at the end of that conflict would have to agree that Collett's caution was perfectly justified.

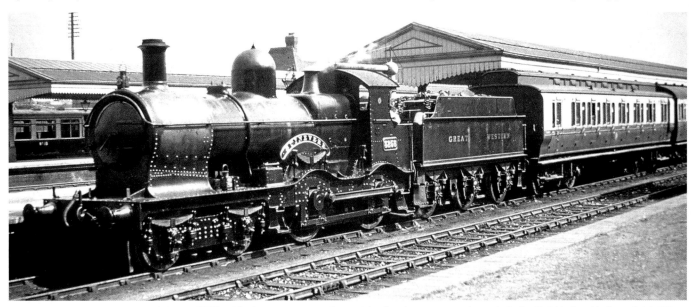

GWR Dean Duke 4-4-0 No 3256 GUINEVERE at Newbury preparing to leave with a Southampton stopping train in April 1939. Outside framed 4-4-0 No 3256 did not become a BR engine *Colour-Rail*

COLLETT'S NAME GAME!

Although described as taciturn and not being overly blessed with an obvious sense of humour one particular act by Collett surely points to a hidden devilish trait! He had no time for anything which he saw as pomposity in general and in particular by the certain directors of the Great Western Railway. A number of the GWR 'great and good' had expressed a desire to have their names carried on company locomotives. Pun certainly intended, as the saying goes 'Every dog must have his day!'

The GWR had taken the decision c1936/37 to combine parts of the extremely old Duke and Bulldog classes to form the 'Earl' or, as the resultant rebuilds became known, Dukedog class of engines. First built in the late 19th century to a design by William Dean the ageing locomotives were reduced to kits of parts and then reassembled at Swindon to emerge in 1936 as a 'new' class. However even though they were fine engines no amount of rebuilding could disguise their obvious 19th century appearance, alongside the Castle and King engines of that time the Dukedogs looked positively ancient.

The 'new' engines were all named after earls in order to supposedly show the 'respect' which the company CME had for the particular directors who had asked for their names to be placed on locomotives, and the titled fraternity in general. At the appointed time the GWR top brass all assembled at Paddington station to witness the arrival of the first 'new' locomotive of the 'Earl' class.

Reports from the time stated that as the mechanically sound, but nevertheless distinctly antiquated-looking engine approached the welcoming party 'a deafening silence descended on the group'. Those directors etc whose names were to be allocated to the Dukedogs were not amused. Collett had his moment, perchance exercising a golden opportunity to deflate what he saw as the GWR balloon of pomposity! Maybe he did have a sense of humour after all? Shortly after the Paddington event, 20 intended Dukedog names were allocated to Castle class locomotives.

CB COLLETT (1871-1952)

Unlike other GWR officials Collett had little truck with civic affairs, but did nominally serve the town of Swindon as a Justice of the Peace from 1921 to 1928 (eg Daniel Gooch was MP for Cricklade and Deputy Lord Lieutenant of Berkshire while Churchward served a spell as Mayor of Swindon). Collett clocked up an amazing total of 48 years at Swindon Works, he retired in 1941 when in his 70th year. Other retired GWR personnel were known to regularly visit the works, not so Collett, upon retirement he virtually severed all links with the company he had served so loyally. His retirement took him to London where he died when aged 81, on 5 April 1952. His funeral was from all accounts a modest affair nevertheless the attendees included his successor Frederick W Hawksworth, former colleague Sir William A Stanier and past GWR General Manager Sir Felix Pole.

Castle class No 5043 EARL OF MOUNT EDGCUMBE was originally built as BARBURY CASTLE and entered GWR service in March 1936, the loco's name was changed in September 1937. The engine is pictured leaving Exeter St David's with a Liverpool-Plymouth service on 23 July 1956. *David Anderson.*

COLLETT LOCOMOTIVES

The GWR locomotive fleet taken into stock by BR was all the better for Collett's influence. Although most commentators pulled up short of calling Collett personally a great designer, all acknowledged his superb engineering and organisational skills. In line with most CMEs he did not necessarily hold the pencil and set square that turned new ideas into steam locomotive designs, but he firmly controlled the team that did. The BR era in the Western Region was dominated by Collett engines and they weren't all express passenger types. In fact the pannier tanks, from five separate classes originated by him, totalled 997 locomotives. Horses, as they say for courses, the GWR/WR had a lot of work which suited pannier tanks.

Collett's first big impact on the GWR was the introduction of his 4073 Castle class 7P four-cylinder 4-6-0 locomotives which were all built at Swindon Works between 1923 and 1951. There were 171 Castles built and the total included 15 engines which were rebuilt from Churchwards Star class and the only GWR Pacific No 111 THE GREAT BEAR. However there were never more than 170 engines in service at any one time as rebuilt Star No 100 A1 LLOYD'S was withdrawn from service almost six months before the last Castle No

7037 SWINDON was completed at the works bearing its name.

Churchward's loco No 111 THE GREAT BEAR was the first Pacific locomotive ever 'steamed' in the UK and the only 4-6-2 ever built by the GWR. Built in 1908 this loco was considered at the time to be the company's flagship engine. The GWR Pacific had 20-ton 9cwt axle load which severely restricted its route availability. In 1924 the Pacific which had been in service for 16 years was in need of attention, and required a new boiler.

Collett decided that it should be rebuilt as a four-cylinder 4-6-0 Castle not as a 4-6-2; not everyone at the GWR agreed with his decision and indeed General Manager Sir Felix Pole personally questioned Collett about it. Justifying his decision on economical grounds Collett pointed out that the engine had steaming problems which would be expensive to cure and being restricted to the London-Bristol route was according to the CME 'a liability not an asset'. Other critics of his decision maintained that the Castle option was the easy option and suggested that Collett had missed the chance of using the 'redundant' 4-6-2 as a test bed for a completely new locomotive design.

GWR Collett Castle No 100 A1 LLOYD'S pictured at Reading with an Up express in April 1947. This loco was introduced in April 1925 and was a Castle rebuilt from Star 4-6-0 No 4009 SHOOTING STAR, renamed and renumbered in January 1936. At that time of this picture the locomotive was configured as an oil burner and the top of the tank can be clearly seen in the tender. *Colour-Rail*

Castle No 100 A1 LLOYD'S was originally built as a Churchward Star class engine No 4009 SHOOTING STAR and was rebuilt as a Castle by Collett. First allocated to Plymouth Laira depot the loco was withdrawn from Old Oak Common (81A).

A rare picture of the first Pacific locomotive ever built in the UK and the only 4-6-2 ever built by the GWR, Churchward's loco No 111 THE GREAT BEAR is seen 'on shed'. No 111 was rebuilt by Collett in 1924 as a Castle class 4-6-0. The engine retained the number 111 and was named VISCOUNT CHURCHILL. *Laurence Waters/Great Western Society*

In 1926 the London Midland and Scottish Railway took loco No 5000 LAUNCESTON CASTLE on loan and the engine was put to work on the West Coast Main Line between London and Carlisle. The locomotive performed well and as a result the LMS are said to have requested the GWR to build a batch of Castles for them to use on their Anglo-Scottish express services. When the GWR declined to accept that order the LMS asked instead for a set of engineering drawings!

That request also fell upon deaf ears but although the LMS did not get the locomotives at that time they did eventually gain the services of a Swindon man who knew all about Castles and Kings! It is interesting to remember that William A Stanier was almost certainly 'looking over Collett's shoulder' during the development of first the Castle class engines and later the King class locomotives. Accordingly the GWR influence in Stanier's LMS designs is there for all to see.

It is a fact that Castles were the backbone of GWR and later WR express services for over 40 years. They were as popular with the men who crewed them in the final years of BR steam as they were with the enginemen of the late 1920s. Castles were put in charge of most of the GWR's crack express services in their heyday, and were to be seen equally at home on services to the holiday resorts of the West Country and expresses to South Wales.

In the late 1920s and early 1930s Castle class engines were in charge of the famous Cheltenham Flyer. Those services called for the locos to average 66.2mph, and allowed just 70 minutes to cover the 77.3 miles from Swindon to Paddington. By modern standards that may not seem a tall order but carried out on a daily basis it was an outstanding achievement of the time, for the locomotives and their footplatemen. There were many instances of Castle class locomotives in charge of heavy trains topping the 100mph mark, even when in their dotage.

Resting between turns at Oxford in May 1961 is GWR Castle No 5082 SWORDFISH and sister engine No 7008 SWANSEA CASTLE. *David Anderson*

Castle No 5082 was originally built as POWIS CASTLE, entering GWR service in June 1939. First shed allocation was Bristol, Bath Road. BR shed allocations included Bristol, Bath Road (82A) and Old Oak Common (81A) from where the engine was withdrawn. Castle No 7008 was built in May 1948 and thus entered service for British Railways Western Region. The loco was first allocated to Oxford (81F) and withdrawn from Old Oak Common (81A).

April 1983 saw preserved Collett Castle class 4-6-0 No 5051 DRYSLLWYN CASTLE (AKA EARL BATHURST) being serviced at Crewe Bank, Shrewsbury, while on 'Welsh Marches Pullman' duty in April 1983. Swindon-built No 5051 is preserved by the Great Western Society, Didcot. *Author*

King No 6027 KING RICHARD 1 pictured at Weston-super-Mare (Locking Road) in September 1937. The driver is oiling around. *Author's Collection*

The first of the class 4073 CAERPHILLY CASTLE was displayed at the 1924 British Empire Exhibition alongside the LNER's FLYING SCOTSMAN. At that time the GWR Castle 4-6-0 was the most powerful locomotive in Britain and after visiting the exhibition Nigel Gresley was reportedly 'very impressed' with the Collett locomotive. Locomotive 4073 was the first of Collett's new class to enter service, it did so on 23 August 1923. The four-cylinder 4-6-0 ran almost two million miles in service before being withdrawn in May 1960, and placed on display at the Science Museum, London.

When Hawksworth became GWR CME he presided over a continuing Castle building programme. In 1948 BR became the builders of the remaining '4073' class locomotive on the order books and they built numbers 7012 to 7037 (26 engines) with 7036 TAUNTON CASTLE and 7037 SWINDON being the last, both completed in August 1950. Withdrawals had started in the same year (among the six ex Star rebuilds) with 4009 SHOOTING STAR being the first in March 1950, the first Castle proper to be scrapped was 5005 MANORBIER CASTLE (built 1927) withdrawn in February 1960, with 1.7 million miles on the clock. The last in service was the 1950-built 7029 CLUN CASTLE withdrawn and preserved in December 1965.

Next Collett locomotives out of 'the works' were the '56xx' 0-6-2T class in 1924 and in that same year the first of the '49xx' Hall class 5MT 4-6-0s entered service; between 1928 and 1943 Swindon built 258 of them, which all passed into BR ownership. The numbers in use of the popular wide route availability mixed traffic type were increased between 1944 and 1950 when GWR under Hawksworth (and then BR) introduced the additional 71 locomotives of the 6959 Modified Hall 5MT 4-6-0 class.

Bottom: **GWR Collett '5600' class 0-6-2T No 6665 trundles by Cardiff Canton with a loaded rake of mineral wagons in March 1959. Built by Armstrong Whitworth & Co Ltd in 1928 this loco was withdrawn by BR in October 1965.** *David Anderson*

In 1927 the GWR board's request for a more powerful locomotive to haul heavier and faster trains was complied with when Collett rolled out the first of his four-cylinder '6000' King Class 8P 4-6-0 locomotives. Named KING GEORGE V that locomotive visited the United States and to this day (in preservation) it carries a donated commemorative bell on the front bufferbeam. The total number built was 30 and the last loco into service was 6029, in August 1930. Initially the 22-ton 10 cwt axle loading of the Kings confined them to the London-Plymouth, London-Bristol and London-Wolverhampton routes. Later after permanent way improvements the class were allowed between Bristol and Shrewsbury and importantly through the Severn Tunnel into Wales.

The 1930s railway love affair with streamlining did not completely pass the GWR by. In keeping with the trend of the time the GWR had a mild flirtation with partial streamlining. King class loco No 6014 KING HENRY VII received a bullet nose and other embellishments thought by many observers to ruin the classical looks of a previously handsome engine. One other loco, Castle class No 5005 MANORBIER CASTLE received similar treatment. Loco No 6014 emerged in 'bullet nose' partial streamlined form from Swindon Works in March 1935, but by January 1943 all signs of the streamlining had been removed apart from the 'V' shaped cab.

The Kings were all withdrawn in 1962 the first being 6006 KING GEORGE I in February of that year. In December the last three were taken out of service, they were 6000 KING GEORGE V, 6018 KING HENRY VI and 6025 KING HENRY III. The Kings were not necessarily taken out of service because their condition warranted it but because diesels had started to replace them on the Western Region's express trains.

In 1936 Collett's '68xx' 5MT Grange 4-6-0 class entered service and 80 were built, the last in 1939. The Grange was basically a version of the Hall class with smaller wheels. The first 20 of the Manor '78xx' class 4-6-0s were built at the same time, with the balance following from BR in 1950. Although also rated at 5MT the Manors were a lighter version of the Grange class, with wider route availability, 30 were built.

A delightfully rural image of GWR/BR WR Collett Manor '7800' class 4-6-0 No 7825 LECHLADE MANOR adjacent to the Down starter at Narbeth with the 10.45 Whitland-Pembroke Dock service, May 1958. Built by BR at Swindon in 1950 this loco was withdrawn in April 1965.
Colour-Rail/Historic Model Railway Society

Castle class No 5005 MANORBIER CASTLE pictured at Tyseley in 1937 with the reportedly unpopular GWR 'bullet nose' streamline embellishments. This historically important image was taken by Brian Dengerfield senior.
Brian Dengerfield Collection

Castle No 5005 entered service for the GWR in June 1927. First shed allocation was Old Oak Common. This loco carried streamlining from March 1935 until 1940. BR shed allocations included Cardiff Canton (86C) and Swindon (82C) from where the locomotive was withdrawn.

Included in the large number of tank locomotives, introduced during Collett's time were 863 members of the '57xx' 3F 0-6-0PT class. The pannier tanks were built between 1929 and 1950 not only at Swindon Works but by outside contractors Armstrong Whitworth, WG Bagnall, Beyer Peacock, Kerr Stewart, North British Locomotive Company and Yorkshire Engine Company.

Castle Builder and King Maker are titles often bestowed upon Collett but the long-serving GWR CME gave us much more. In addition to improvements in railway safety, better rolling stock and cutting edge manufacturing techniques he is credited with the design of 15 new locomotive classes which resulted in 2281 new locomotives being built during the steam era, by both the GWR and British Railways. In the same period he supervised the rebuilding/improvement of eight classes

of locomotives totalling some 308 engines. A Collett combined total of 2589 locomotives by any standard can be considered a formidable contribution to British steam locomotive building. As a comparison the great Sir Nigel Gresley was associated with the design and building of 1621 locomotives, while Sir William A Stanier had 2431 locomotives attributed to him during his term as a CME.

There are a total of 138 preserved ex GWR/BR WR steam locomotives and given the statistics quoted above it will come as no surprise to readers that 101 of those are from designs/ improvements attributable to one Charles Benjamin Collett OBE (1871-1952). To many younger enthusiasts, who have only experienced GWR locomotive types on preserved railways the name Collett is rightly synonymous with the Great Western Railway!

A typical 1961 GWR scene, this image was taken at the east end of Oxford station. Collett/Hawksworth Modified Hall No 7904 FOUNTAINS HALL stands alongside Collett Castle No 7005 SIR EDWARD ELGAR which had just arrived with a Hereford and Worcester to Paddington express service. *David Anderson*

Castle No 7005 was originally named LAMPHEY CASTLE and entered GWR service in June 1946. The locomotive's first and last shed allocation was Worcester (85A).

Preserved Castle class No 5051 seen at Didcot and named as EARL BATHURST; built in 1936 this locomotive was originally named DRYSLLWYN CASTLE, a name which it has carried in preservation. *Author*

Castle No 7031 CROMWELL'S CASTLE was built by British Railways and entered service in June 1950. In this 1960s picture the engine is seen at speed on the 'Didcot Avoiding Line' (East). *David Anderson*

Castle No 5003 LULWORTH CASTLE (then a Newton Abbot allocated loco) is pictured in the summer of 1961. The location is Didcot as the Hawksworth tendered 4-6-0 sets out for the West Country with a train of milk empties from Kensington, a job for which Castle engines were often rostered. There is much railway detail to enjoy in this delightfully period image, signals, S&T location cabinet, water column, PW trolley, track chairs and worn out wooden sleepers etc. *David Anderson.*

Loco No 5003 entered service in May 1927 and was first allocated to Old Oak Common depot. Allocations under BR included Taunton (83B) and Newton Abbot (83A) from where the engine was withdrawn in 1962.

Castle class No 7013 BRISTOL CASTLE seen under the signal gantry at Oxford station with the Down 'Cathedrals Express' on 16 June 1962. The end was fast approaching, note the DMU on the left. *David Anderson*

Preserved King class No 6024 KING EDWARD 1 is pictured on the turntable at Tyseley on 3 October 2004. *Brian Wilson*

Castles in the Night'. An evocative study of two Tyseley-based Castle class engines 'on shed'. No 7029 CLUN CASTLE with a GWR-style tender and No

BRITAIN'S MOST POWERFUL EXPRESS PASSENGER LOCOMOTIVES

Locomotive No 4000 NORTH STAR was first built by the GWR in 1906 as No 40, a 4-4-2 Atlantic and subsequently rebuilt in as a Star class 4-6-0 engine in 1909 and named NORTH STAR. Rebuilt for a second time as a 4-6-0 Castle, the loco then re-entered service in November 1929. The engine is pictured at Wolverhampton Stafford Road in March 1956, coupled with a Hawksworth tender.
Colour-Rail/ K Cooper

Withdrawn by British Railways in May 1957, No 4000 ran over 2.1-million miles in GWR and BR WR service before being cut up at Swindon Works. NORTH STAR noticeably had a short chimney and large front cab windows. Additionally, No 4000 retained its original (Atlantic) frame with footplating 2 ½ inches higher than all the other Star and Castle class locomotives. As a Castle, NORTH STAR was first allocated to Newton Abbot depot and under BR saw service from Wolverhampton Stafford Road (84A) and Swansea Landore (87E) from where the loco was withdrawn.

THE FIRST CASTLE

CB Collett's first 4073 Castle class four-cylinder 4-6-0 locomotive No 4073 CAERPHILLY CASTLE was introduced to the public at Paddington Station on 23 August 1923. The new class was initially developed to handle increased traffic and heavier trains on the long non-stop runs between London Paddington and Plymouth. The class was proclaimed by the GWR as being 'Britain's most powerful express passenger locomotive', notwithstanding the fact that the Collett design was seen as a direct development of GJ Churchward's earlier Star class.

The Castle class was Great Western Railway Chief Mechanical Engineer's first 4-6-0 locomotive which when exhibited at the British Empire Exhibition at Wembley in 1924 received almost unreserved acclaim. In fact, No 4073 was exhibited alongside Gresley's 4-6-2 No 4472 FLYING SCOTSMAN, as a result of which trials between the two types were later held, in which the Castle proved to be the superior engine. Thereafter, the London North Eastern Railway (LNER) Pacifics were modified in order to take account of the lessons learned.

Right: **GWR Castle 4-6-0 No 4073 CAERPHILLY CASTLE is pictured at Cardiff Canton depot (86C) on 28 June 1958.** *Colour-Rail/K Fairley*

Loco No 4073 at that time still retained original GWR-style tapered buffers, valve spindle covers and tender; the loco was never fitted with a double chimney. When entering traffic in August 1923, the loco was allocated to Old Oak Common depot; under BR allocations for the engine included Bristol Bath Road (82A) and Cardiff Canton (86A) from where the loco was withdrawn in 1960.

POWER PERSONIFIED

The Castle locomotives were in the region of 10 per cent more powerful than the Star class engines and in order to provide that power, the cylinders were increased from 15-inch diameter (of the Star class) to 16-inch diameter and additionally a larger boiler was developed. With working boiler pressure maintained at 225lb per square inch, the Castle engines could deliver a tractive effort of 31,625lb at 85 per cent boiler pressure against the Star's 27,800lb. Importantly, Collett's four-cylinder 4-6-0 design accommodated within it the maximum 20-ton axle loading (over a 14 foot 9 inch driving wheel base) demanded of him by the then in force GWR permanent way restrictions, compared with the final Star class axle loading of 19.4

tons. Churchward's Star class engines had driving wheels of 6 foot 8 ½ inch diameter, that dimension was also selected by Collett for his Castle class.

In overall dimensions, the Castle class locomotives were only 12 inches longer that their predecessors but had a much better appointed cab than the Star engines, incorporating side windows and an extended roof; for the driver and fireman, the added luxury of tip-up seats! The Castles were very handsome locomotives when turned out of Swindon's famous 'A Shop' in traditional GWR Brunswick Green, with copper-topped chimney, polished brass safety valve covers, polished brass splasher beadings, lined-out panels and boiler bands.

Opposite: **Three preserved Castle class locomotives displayed adjacent to the turntable at the Tyseley Open Day 29 June 2008. Left to right No 5029 NUNNEY CASTLE, No 5043 EARL OF MOUNT EDGCUMBE (AKA BARBURY CASTLE) then only partly restored and No 7029 CLUN CASTLE.**
Brian Wilson

31

To celebrate CAERPHILLY CASTLE being placed on display at Wembley, a jigsaw puzzle entitled 'Build the Caerphilly Castle' was put on sale by the GWR, and was very favourably received. Any person lucky enough to own one in good condition now has in their possession a very collectable item! To further promote the engine, thousands of postcard and cigarette card images of No 4073 were produced. Indeed a GWR 1924 publication entitled A Book of Railway Locomotives for Boys of All Ages featuring the Castle by WG Chapman and priced at one shilling (five new pence), incredibly sold some 60,000 copies in a couple of months (now valued as collectors' items).

Nine more Castle class locomotives were built from December 1923 onwards and by April 1924 the GWR had 10 of the class in service. Swindon generally built the Castle class 4-6-0s in batches of 10 locomotives with the 16 rebuilt Star class engines fitted in between in no particular order but more or less as Stars became due for new cylinders and boilers. Also rebuilt as a Castle, on Collett's instructions, was the only ever GWR Pacific (also the first of that wheel arrangement to be built in Britain) locomotive No 111 THE GREAT BEAR which entered traffic as a Castle in September 1924, retaining its original number but being renamed VISCOUNT CHURCHILL.

One happy boy! A young footplate visitor is seen on Castle No 5047 EARL OF DARTMOUTH at Wolverhampton Low Level station in 1960. Note that the Hawksworth tender has a mixed load of coal and 'ovoids'. *Author's Collection*

Loco No 5047 EARL OF DARTMOUTH was originally built as COMPTON CASTLE, and entered GWR service in April 1936. This was one of 23 Castles renamed as Earls in 1937. This engine was first allocated to Swansea Landore depot. BR allocations for this engine included Newton Abbot (83A) and Wolverhampton, Stafford Road (84A) from where the loco was withdrawn in September 1962.

Preserved Castle No 5043 EARL OF MOUNT EDGCUMBE is pictured at Tyseley 25 October 2009. First named BARBURY CASTLE, the loco is often seen carrying that name in preservation. *Brian Wilson*

Initially four Stars were rebuilt between 1925 and 1926 while 30 actual Castle class engines were built before the next Star was converted in 1929. That engine was No 4000 NORTH STAR which started life as Churchward's first four-cylinder engine, a 4-4-2 Atlantic built in 1906 and then converted to a Star in 1909. The Star to Castle conversions required a new section to be added to the locomotives' frames, behind the trailing wheels, in order to accommodate the larger Castle firebox and cab, with a new boiler and cylinders also provided. Even though the old Star valve gear, motion and wheels were reused, the resultant Castle engines could effectively be considered as being 'new'.

Castle No 4084
ABERYSTWYTH CASTLE
is pictured 'on shed' at Bristol
Bath Road (82A) in May 1953.
Colour-Rail

As pictured, the loco has parallel buffers but original GWR tender and valve spindle covers. The loco entered service in May 1925 and was first allocated to Plymouth Laira depot. Shed allocations under BR included Bristol Bath Road (82A), Newton Abbot (83A) and Cardiff Canton (86C) from where the engine was withdrawn in 1960.

LOCOMOTIVE TRIALS

Details of the aforementioned 1925 locomotive trials with the LNER are as follows. Loco No 4079 PENDENNIS CASTLE went to the LNER and worked trains on the East Coat Main Line out of King's Cross in a direct comparison with Gresley Pacifics No 4475 FLYING FOX and No 2545 DIAMOND JUBILEE; also LNER loco No 4474 VICTOR WILD was temporally allocated to Old Oak Common in order to work 'against' No 4074 CALDICOT CASTLE on the Paddington-Plymouth route.

Although during the exchanges, all the locomotives concerned performed their allocated tasks with credibility, the GWR locomotives were judged to have been the most successful overall when taking into account coal consumption and general performance. In fairness, it must be pointed out that the LNER soon after put into practice all the lessons learned from the trials, and their later-built Pacifics were the better engines for it.

In 1926, the London Midland & Scottish Railway (LMSR), for the purpose of evaluation, 'borrowed' loco No 5000 LAUNCESTON CASTLE which they trialled on the West Coast Main Line. The success of that venture led to the LMSR asking Swindon to build 50 Castle class engines for their use. Famously the GWR declined to do so.

Loco No 5006 TREGENNA CASTLE underlined the all-round capabilities of the class when on 6 June 1932 the engine made its famous run on the 'Cheltenham Flyer' during which the 77.3 miles from Swindon to Paddington were covered in 56 minutes 47 seconds while hauling a train of 186 tons and attaining a maximum speed of 92mph. Five years later, No 5039 RHUDDLAN CASTLE turned in an even better performance on the same service but with a train of 223 tons, recording a maximum speed of 95mph. The first occasion when a Castle was officially recorded at a speed of 100mph was in 1939 when loco No 4086 BUILTH CASTLE went 'ton up' down Honeybourne Bank.

Below: **Castle No 5076 GLADIATOR was originally named DRYSLLWYN CASTLE. The loco is seen with a Hawksworth tender, BR-style parallel buffer barrels and valve spindle covers.**

Loco No 5076 GLADIATOR entered GWR service in August 1938. This was one of 12 Castle class engines renamed after World War Two aircraft in 1940/41. The loco was first allocated to Exeter depot. BR allocations included Bristol, Bath Road (82A) and Southall (81C) from where the loco was withdrawn in 1964.

Castle No 5097 SARUM CASTLE is pictured marshalling passenger stock at Oxford prior to a departure to Paddington with an express service in August 1961.
This profile of the loco shows the double chimney to good effect. Note also the GWR-style tender but BR pattern parallel buffer barrels. *David Anderson*

Loco No 5097 entered GWR service in July 1939 and was first allocated to Shrewsbury depot. BR allocations for this loco included Cardiff Canton (86C) and Cardiff East Dock (88L) from where the engine was withdrawn in September 1962.

Castle No 4074 CALDICOT CASTLE took part in trials against LNER loco No 4474 VICTOR WILD on the Paddington-Plymouth route. The smartly turned out loco is seen passing Didcot at speed on the Oxford line with a Paddington-Worcester Hereford service in August 1962. *David Anderson*

On entering service in December 1923, No 4074 was first allocated to Old Oak Common depot. BR allocations for this loco included a spell at Swansea Landore depot.

Castle No 4079 PENDENNIS CASTLE went to the LNER and worked trains on the East Coat Main Line out of King's Cross in a direct comparison with Gresley Pacifics No 4475 FLYING FOX and No 2545 DIAMOND JUBILEE. The engine is pictured prior to being shipped to a purchaser in Australia. *Author.*

LAST STAR CONVERTS

Between 1937 and 1940, the last 10 Star class engines (4063-72) were converted to Castles bringing the total number of the class in service to 130 by the end of 1940. They were numbers 111, 4009, 4016, 4032, 4037 and 4073 to 5097. No more Castle class engines were built under the reign of CB Collett who retired from the GWR in 1941. Collett was succeeded by FW Hawksworth who recommenced building further members of the class in May 1946 with engine No 5098 CLIFFORD CASTLE. During this period, the GWR experimented with 'Bullet Nosed Streamlining' and No 5005 MANORBIER CASTLE was one of the two locomotives chosen to carry embellishments designed to improve air flow over the engine at speed.

No 5098 together with other members of the 1946 batch of 10 engines (5098-5099 and 7000-7007) marked the introduction by Hawksworth of a three-row superheater in place of the as-designed two-row version. That modification led to No 5098 being talked of as the best Castle class locomotive ever built. That claim was however relatively short-lived, as in 1947 Hawksworth went a stage further by rebuilding No 5049 EARL OF PLYMOUTH with a new boiler incorporating a four-row superheater. Thereafter, claims of economy in water consumption, prolonged boiler life and greatly reduced maintenance justified building all future Castle boilers to that configuration.

Above: **Preserved Castle class loco No 5051 EARL BATHURST is pictured on shed at Neath depot (87A) in August 1961. No 5051 was originally named DRYSLLWYN CASTLE. The loco is coupled to a Hawksworth tender and has parallel buffers and BR-style valve spindle covers.**
Colour-Rail

Left: **Castle No 7030 CRANBROOK CASTLE was from the last batch of BR-built locomotives and is pictured leaving Swindon with a down train in October 1959.**
Colour-Rail/PJ Hughes

Loco No 7030 entered British Railways service in June 1960 and was first allocated to Old Oak Common (81A) from where the locomotive was withdrawn in 1963.

BRITISH RAILWAYS

As building of the class continued, British Railways (Western Region) superseded the Great Western Railway (January 1948) and the first Castle built under BR was No 7008 SWANSEA CASTLE. A total of 10 Castle class engines were built in 1948 (7008-7017), a further 10 in 1949 (7018-7027), and the last 10 in 1950 (7028-7037). In all, 171 Castle class engines entered service for the GWR and BR WR but the highest total in service at any one time was only 170, as the first Castle was withdrawn before the last built example entered service. All of the class were built at Swindon Works.

All of the class were given names and a great deal of 'actual' re-naming took place with 28 engines being renamed between 1936 and 1938, 12 renamed 1940/41, two renamed in 1954 and one loco renamed in 1957. Making up the list of 'final' names were 112 Castles, 21 Earls, 12 WW2 aircraft, nine Abbeys, eight individuals or organisations including Great Western, three Regiments, three Viscounts, one Queen, one Star and the last built Castle Swindon.

Loco No 7013 built as BRISTOL CASTLE in 1948 was re-named and re-numbered 4082 WINDSOR CASTLE in February 1952, with the original WINDSOR CASTLE becoming No 7013. The identity swap came about at the time of the funeral of King George VI on 15 February 1952. Loco No 4082 WINDSOR CASTLE was requested to haul the funeral train from Paddington to Windsor as the late King had once driven the engine on a visit to Swindon Works. However, at that time, the loco was undergoing a 'heavy' repair in Swindon Works and as a consequence her plates were switched with No 7013, and the locomotives' identities were never changed back!

Right: **Castle class No 5069 ISAMBARD KINGDOM BRUNEL pictured in 1957 at Penzance waiting to depart with the Up Cornish Riviera.** *Colour-Rail/J Spencer Gilks collection.*

Loco No 5090 was a re-built from Star class engine with the original name NEATH ABBEY which entered GWR service in April 1939 and was first allocated to Plymouth Laira depot. BR shed allocations included Bristol, Bath Road (82A) and Old Oak Common (81A) from where the engine was withdrawn in May 1962.

Castle No 7013 BRISTOL CASTLE pictured at Shrewsbury with a 'Cambrian Coast Express' headboard. Note that in this image the loco has original GWR-style tapered buffers and tender, but new-style piston valve covers and double chimney; this locomotive was originally No 4082 WINDSOR CASTLE. *Colour-Rail*

The first shed allocation for this engine was Old Oak Common (81A). After being renumbered as 4082, the loco was also for a time allocated to Gloucester (85B) and was withdrawn from Old Oak Common in 1965.

Castle class No 5048 EARL OF DEVON is pictured at Exeter St David's station waiting to depart with an Up Paddington/Bristol express service on 10 June 1955. *David Anderson*

Loco No 5048 was originally built as CRANBROOK CASTLE and entered GWR service in April 1936, being first allocated to Bristol, Bath Road depot. The engine was renamed in August 1937. BR shed allocations included included Bristol, Bath Road (82A) and Llanelly (87F) from where the loco was withdrawn in August 1962.

Castle class engines continued to impress in service and over time were allowed to run over all the GWR main lines and thus became the company's standard express passenger engine class. A GWR Star in tip-top order could handle a train of 15 coaches and keep to schedule, but without any power in reserve with which to recover from unforeseen adverse conditions. As the more powerful, sure-footed Castles took over previous Star duties, they easily provided that margin.

Most of the regular work allocated to the class involved hauling trains of between 10 and 12 coaches. Indeed, on the Bristol route, the GWR fixed a train tare weight of 455 tons for the Castle class which was equivalent to 14 of the heaviest bogie coaches of the time. That loading compared favourably with the King class locomotives which on similar routes were permitted to load to 15 bogies, while still operating within accepted margins.

Castle No 5058 EARL OF CLANCARTY pictured at Aller with an 18.10 Goodrington to Plymouth service in July 1961. *Colour-Rail/PW Gray*

Loco No 5058 was originally built as NEWPORT CASTLE (renamed 1937) and entered service in May 1937 when allocated to Newton Abbott. British Railways allocations for the loco included Plymouth Laira (84A) and Gloucester (85B) from where the engine was withdrawn in 1963.

After extensive trials on the test bed at Swindon loco, No 7018 DRYSLLWYN CASTLE was selected for further development, becoming the first of the class to be fitted with an experimental double chimney in May 1956, but retaining a three-row superheater. The final development of the class was almost complete when loco No 4090 DORCHESTER CASTLE (the second engine fitted with a double chimney) was given a boiler with a four-row superheater.

The loco was described by observers of the time as a 'remarkable engine' and her performances hauling the 'Bristolian' certainly justified that claim. However, in 1958, the ultimate Castle class development took place when loco No 7018 DRYSLLWYN CASTLE was further modified by the addition of a four-row superheater and a newly developed mechanical lubricator which the engineers claimed would deliver 50 per cent more oil than was previously achievable.

This image of Preserved Castle No 7029 CLUN CASTLE shows the pleasing lines of the class design to great effect. This loco had the benefit of British Railways' final modifications which included a boiler with four-row superheater and double chimney and mechanical lubricator. The loco has enjoyed a very successful life in preservation and in 2010 was the subject of an appeal to once again put this iconic locomotive back into steam. *Phil Neale*

The Western Region of BR wanted to cut the journey time of the 'Bristolian' and loco No 7018 was chosen to complete the run. On 28 April 1958, the engine made a record run which included 100mph at Somerford with an actual start to stop time of 93 minutes 50 seconds for the 117.6 miles from Bristol to Paddington, with a seven-coach train. That impressive performance beat by almost two minutes the best time recorded on the route by a King class engine. A week later, No 7018, with the same Bristol Bath Road footplateman in charge, equalled her own record, but on that occasion did so with an eight-coach train.

It is fortunate that a total of eight Collett Castle 4073 class locomotives survived into preservation, comprising two locomotives of 1924 vintage, one from 1934, two each from 1936 and 1939, one from 1949 and one from the final 1950 batch of engines.

GREAT WESTERN RAILWAY COLLETT CASTLE 4073 CLASS DETAILS	
Power Classification:	6P reclassified 7P by British Railways in 1951
GWR Power Class:	D
GWR Axle Load code:	Red
Introduced:	1923-1950
Designer:	Charles Benjamin Collett
Builders:	Swindon Works GWR and BR WR
Total Weight (working):	126 tons 11 cwt
Driving Wheel:	6 foot 8 ½ inches
Leading Wheel:	3 foot 2 inches
Overall length:	65 foot 2 inches (over buffers)
Width:	8 foot 11 inches
Height:	13 foot 4 ½ inches
Boiler Pressure:	225psi superheated
Boiler Type:	No 8
Fire Grate Area:	29.36 square feet
Cylinders:	Four 16 inch diameter x 26 inch stroke
Tractive Effort:	31,625lbf (at 85 per cent boiler pressure)
Valve Gear:	Inside Walschaert with rocking shafts to outside motion (piston valves)
Coal capacity:	6 tons
Water Capacity:	3500 gallons, in 1927 4000* gallon tenders were introduced

171 engines built, GWR and BR WR number series,
111, 4000/4009/4016/4032/4037. 4073-4099. 5000-5099. 7000-7037.

Castle No 7007 GREAT WESTERN is pictured under repair at Plymouth Laira depot (83D) in this 1960 image. Note that the front driving wheels motion and springs have been removed as has the top washout plug. *Author's Collection*

Castle 4-6-0 No 7011 **BANBURY CASTLE** is pictured making a smart getaway from Oxford station with an 8.26pm express service to London Paddington on 13 July 1961. *David Anderson.*

Loco No 7011 entered service in June 1948 and was therefore a British Railways-built engine. First shed allocation for this loco was Bristol, Bath Road (82A) and the last allocation was to Wolverhampton Oxley (84B) from where the engine was withdrawn in 1965.

SUMMARY OF CASTLE CLASS LOCOMOTIVES

NO	NAME	DATE REBUILT	WITHDRAWN	MILEAGE
111	VISCOUNT CHURCHILL P	9/1924	7/1953 (83D)	1,989,628*
4000	NORTH STAR S	11/1929	5/1957 (87E)	2,110,396
4009	SHOOTING STAR S	4/1925	3/1950 (81A)	1,164,297*
4016	KNIGHT OF THE GOLDEN FLEECE S	10/1925	9/1951 (81A)	1,186,663*
4032	QUEEN ALEXANDRA S	4/1926	9/1951 (83B)	1,225,908*
4037	QUEEN PHILIPPA S	6/1926	9/1962 (83C)	1,652,958*

*As a 'Castle' class engine.

RENAMED LOCOMOTIVES

4009   Renumbered **100A1** and renamed LLOYD'S 1/1936

4016   THE SOMERSET LIGHT INFANTRY (PRINCE ALBERT'S) 1/1938

4037   THE SOUTH WALES BORDERERS 3/1937

S- Rebuilt 'Star' class engines. P-Rebuilt from Pacific locomotive THE GREAT BEAR, retained the same number.

DISPOSAL

111   Swindon Works

4000   Swindon Works

100 A1 Swindon Works

4016   Swindon Works

4032   Swindon Works

4037   Cashmores, Newport

Castle class No 4037 THE SOUTH WALES BORDERERS is pictured at Newton Abbot station in May 1958 while Grange No 6849 WALTON GRANGE can be seen to the right. *Colour-Rail/K Fairley*

No 4037 was originally rebuilt as QUEEN PHILIPPA from Star class engine of same name and number, entered GWR service in June 1926. First shed allocation Wolverhampton. BR shed allocations included Old Oak Common (81A) Newton Abbot (83A) and Exeter (83C) from where the loco was withdrawn.

NO	NAME	DATE BUILT	WITHDRAWN	DOUBLE CHIMNEY	MILEAGE
4073	CAERPHILLY CASTLE	8/1923	5/1960 (86C)	-	1,910,730
4074	CALDICOT CASTLE	12/1923	5/1963 (81A)	4/1959	1,844,072
4075	CARDIFF CASTLE	1/1924	11/1961(81A)	-	1,807,802
4076	CARMARTHEN CASTLE	2/1924	2/1963 (87F)	-	1,697,895
4077	CHEPSTOW CASTLE	2/1924	8/1962 (82B)	-	1,823,488
4078	PEMBROKE CASTLE	2/1924	7/1962 (87F)	-	1,917,380

DISPOSAL

4073	**Preserved**
4074	Swindon Works
4075	Swindon Works
4076	Hayes, Bridgend
4077	Cashmores, Newport
4078	Hayes, Bridgend

Castle class loco No 4073 **CAERPHILLY CASTLE is pictured at Staircross station with a Down passenger train on 25 July 1956.** *David Anderson*

Loco No 4073 (the first Castle proper) entered GWR service in August 1923, and was exhibited at the 1924 British Empire Exhibition at Wembley. The loco was first allocated to Old Oak Common depot. Withdrawn in May 1960 for preservation the engine was first cosmetically restored and initially placed on display at the Science Museum, Kensington, London. Now relocated, iconic loco No 4037 is displayed at Swindon Steam Railway Museum.

NO	NAME	DATE BUILT	WITHDRAWN	DOUBLE CHIMNEY	MILEAGE
4079	PENDENNIS CASTLE	2/1924	5/1964 (82B)	-	1,758,398
4080	POWDERHAM CASTLE	3/1924	8/1964 (81C)	8/1958	1,974,461
4081	WARWICK CASTLE	3/1924	1/1963 (87G)	-	1,894,998
4082	WINDSOR CASTLE	4/1924	9/1964 (85B)	-	712,286*
4083	ABBOTSBURY CASTLE	5/1925	12/1961(88A)	-	1,677,060
4084	ABERYSTWYTH CASTLE	5/1925	10/1960 (86C)	-	1,674,812

*Locomotive No 4082 renumbered 7013 and renamed BRISTOL CASTLE 2/1952. See also mileage for 7013.

DISPOSAL	
4079	**Preserved**
4080	Cashmores, Newport
4081	Hayes, Bridgend
4082	Cashmores, Newport
4083	Swindon Works
4084	Swindon Works

Castle No 4083 ABBOTSBURY CASTLE is pictured at rest in this 1960s image. *Author's Collection*

This loco entered GWR service in May 1925 and was allocated to Old Oak Common depot. BR shed allocations included Newton Abbot (83A) and Cardiff Canton (88A formerly 86C) from where the engine was withdrawn.

Above: Time for a smoke before the off! Loco No 4084 ABERYSTWYTH CASTLE is seen at Exeter St David's Station on 6 June 1955.
David Anderson

Left: Almost departure time! Loco No 4084 prepares to depart the station.
David Anderson

Loco No 4084 entered GWR service in May 1925 and was first allocated to Plymouth Laira depot. BR shed allocations for this engine included Bristol, Bath Road (82A) Newton Abbot (83A) and Cardiff Canton (86C) from where the engine was withdrawn in October 1960.

NO	NAME	DATE BUILT	WITHDRAWN	DOUBLE CHIMNEY	MILEAGE
4085	BERKELEY CASTLE	5/1925	5/1962 (81A)	-	1,651,000
4086	BUILTH CASTLE	6/1925	4/1962 (81F)	-	1,791,633 *
4087	CARDIGAN CASTLE	6/1925	10/1963(82B)	2/1958	1,812,341
4088	DARTMOUTH CASTLE	7/1925	5/1964 (82B)	5/1958	1,848,430
4089	DONNINGTON CASTLE	7/1925	10/1964(81D)	-	1,876,807
4090	DORCHESTER CASTLE	7/1925	6/1963 (88B)	3/1957	1,848,646

*First of the class to officially record a speed of 100mph.

DISPOSAL

4085	Cashmores, Newport
4086	Cashmores, Newport
4087	Coopers Metals Ltd, Sharpness
4088	Cohens, Morriston
4089	Hayes, Bridgend
4090	Cashmores, Newport

NO	NAME	DATE BUILT	WITHDRAWN	DOUBLE CHIMNEY	MILEAGE
4091	DUDLEY CASTLE	7/1925	1/1959(81A)	-	1,691,856
4092	DUNRAVEN CASTLE	8/1925	12/1961(81F)	-	1,718,879
4093	DUNSTER CASTLE	5/1926	9/1964 (85B)	12/1957	1,842,985
4094	DYNEVOR CASTLE	5/1926	3/1962 (87G)	-	1,881,886
4095	HARLECH CASTLE	6/1926	12/1962(81D)	-	1,695,899
4096	HIGHCLERE CASTLE	6/1926	1/1963 (87F)	-	1,958,378

DISPOSAL

4091	Swindon Works
4092	Swindon Works
4093	Cashmores, Newport
4094	Swindon Works
4095	King's, Norwich
4096	Hayes, Bridgend

NO	NAME	DATE BUILT	WITHDRAWN	DOUBLE CHIMNEY	MILEAGE
4097	KENILWORTH CASTLE	6/1926	5/1960 (87E)	6/1958	1,713,966
4098	KIDWELLY CASTLE	7/1926	12/1963(81A)	-	1,723,879
4099	KILGERRAN CASTLE	8/1926	9/1962 (87F)	-	1,873,985
5000	LAUNCESTON CASTLE	9/1926	10/1964(84B)	-	1,870,200*
5001	LLANDOVERY CASTLE	9/1926	2/1963 (81A)	7/1961	1,855,495
5002	LUDLOW CASTLE	9/1926	9/1964 (81C)	-	1,817,218

*Loaned to LMS in 1962 for trials Euston-Carlisle. Mileage up to 1963 only thereafter (84B) became (2B) LMR.

DISPOSAL

4097	Swindon Works
4098	Cashmores, Great Bridge
4099	Hayes, Bridgend
5000	Birds, Morriston
5001	Cashmores, Great Bridge
5002	Hayes, Bridgend

Old Oak Common allocated Castle No 5001 LLANDOVERY CASTLE is pictured in ex works condition at Didcot. Note the later design square inside cylinder box compared to the original (and ex Star) rounded shape. See previous picture of loco No 4083 in this chapter. *David Anderson*

Loco No 5001 entered GWR service in September 1926 and was first allocated to Old Oak Common depot. This engine was experimentally fitted with 6ft 6in driving wheels (instead of 6ft 81/2in) in 1931 to investigate gain in performance, however was refitted with original wheels within weeks. BR shed allocations for this loco included Cardiff Canton (86C) Shrewsbury (84G) and Old Oak Common (81A) from where the engine was withdrawn in February 1963.

NO	NAME	DATE BUILT	WITHDRAWN	DOUBLE CHIMNEY	MILEAGE
5003	LULWORTH CASTLE	5/1927	8/1962(83A)	-	1,698,751
5004	LLANSTEPHAN CASTLE	6/1927	4/1962(87A)	-	1,854,704
5005	MANORBIER CASTLE	6/1927	2/1960(82C)	-	1,731,868 *
5006	TREGENNA CASTLE	6/1927	4/1962(87G)	-	1,812,966
5007	ROUGEMONT CASTLE	6/1927	9/1962(85B)	-	1,854,951
5008	RAGLAN CASTLE	6/1927	9/1962(81A)	3/1961	1,798,646

*Streamlined 1935 to 1943.

DISPOSAL	
5003	Cashmores, Newport
5004	Swindon Works
5005	Swindon Works
5006	Cashmores, Newport
5007	Cashmores, Newport
5008	Cashmores, Great Bridge

Below: **Using the copy of this 1908 map kindly supplied by Brian Wilson of Vintage Trains Ltd, we are able to pinpoint the exact location of No 5005 when this picture was taken. The red square marks the spot of the loco and the carriages in the shot can clearly be placed in the carriage sidings above the engine loop lines.**

Tyseley Locomotive Works & Depot 1908

Castle No 5005 MANORBIER CASTLE is pictured 'on shed' at Tyseley (84E) in May 1958, this loco was one of two GWR engines which were experimentally streamlined (1935-45) and it was the first Castle proper to be scrapped. *Author's Collection*

NO	NAME	DATE BUILT	WITHDRAWN	DOUBLE CHIMNEY	MILEAGE
5009	SHREWSBURY CASTLE	6/1927	10/1960(82C)	-	1,708,246
5010	RESTORMEL CASTLE	7/1927	10/1959(81D)	-	1,684,146
5011	TINTAGEL CASTLE	7/1927	9/1962 (81A)	-	1,732,565
5012	BERRY POMEROY CASTLE	7/1927	4/1962 (81F)	-	1,625,965
5013	ABERGAVENNY CASTLE	6/1932	7/1962 (87A)	-	1,525,662
5014	GOODRICH CASTLE	6/1932	2/1965 (84E)	-	1,665,297*

*Up to December 1963 only thereafter (84E) became (2A) LMR.

DISPOSAL

5009	Swindon Works
5010	Swindon Works
5011	Cashmores, Great Bridge
5012	Cashmores, Newport
5013	Hayes, Bridgend
5014	Cashmores, Great Bridge

Castle No 5012 BERRY POMEROY CASTLE prepares to leave Oxford station with a Paddington-Hereford/Worcester express service in July 1961. *David Anderson.*

Loco No 5012 entered GWR service in July 1927 and was first allocated to Newton Abbot depot. Shed allocations under BR included Plymouth Laira (84A) and Oxford (81F) from where the engine was withdrawn in April 1962.

Preserved Castle No 5029 NUNNEY CASTLE pictured on 'The Shakespeare Express' passing Churchill Cottage on the climb out of Stratford towards Wilmcote on 27 July 2008. *Matthew Wilson*

'The Shakespeare Express' is a popular steam-hauled service operated by Vintage Trains Ltd using restored preserved locomotives and special coaching stock. The service normally operates on Sundays during July, August and early September with two trains in each direction being run. The route serves Birmingham, Tyseley, Henley in Arden and Stratford-upon Avon and several on-train dining options are available. Prominent among the many different types of locomotives used on this service in the past have been Castle class engines No 5029 and No 5043 and King class No 6024. For more information visit www.shakespeareexpress.com

NO	NAME	DATE BUILT	WITHDRAWN	DOUBLE CHIMNEY	MILEAGE
5015	KINGSWEAR CASTLE	7/1932	4/1963 (88B)	-	1,554,288
5016	MONTGOMERY CASTLE	7/1932	9/1962 (87F)	1/1961	1,480,896
5017	ST DONATS CASTLE	7/1932	9/1962 (85B)	-	1,598,851*
5018	ST MAWES CASTLE	7/1932	3/1964 (81D)	-	1,503,642
5019	TREAGO CASTLE	7/1932	9/1962 (84A)	2/1961	1,521,335
5020	TREMATON CASTLE	7/1932	11/1962(87F)	-	1,636,749

*Locomotive No 5017 renamed THE GLOUCESTERSHIRE REGIMENT 28th 61st on 4/1954

DISPOSAL

5015	Central Wagon Co, Ince
5016	Cashmores, Newport
5017	Cashmores, Newport
5018	Cohens, Kettering
5019	Swindon Works
5020	Swindon Works

NO	NAME	DATE BUILT	WITHDRAWN	DOUBLE CHIMNEY	MILEAGE
5021	WHITTINGTON CASTLE	8/1932	9/1962 (86C)	-	1,446,936
5022	WIGMORE CASTLE	8/1932	6/1963 (84A)	3/1959	1,546,104
5023	BRECON CASTLE	4/1934	2/1963 (82C)	-	1,479,168
5024	CAREW CASTLE	4/1934	5/1962 (83A)	-	1,351,161
5025	CHIRK CASTLE	4/1934	11/1963 (85C)	-	1,401,530
5026	CRICCIETH CASTLE	4/1934	11/1964 (84B)	10/1959	1,209,487*

*Until December 1963 only thereafter (84B) became (2B) LMR.

DISPOSAL

5021	Cashmores, Newport
5022	Cashmores, Great Bridge
5023	Swindon Works
5024	Cashmores, Newport
5025	Cashmores, Great Bridge
5026	Cashmores, Great Bridge

NO	NAME	DATE BUILT	WITHDRAWN	DOUBLE CHIMNEY	MILEAGE
5027	FARLEIGH CASTLE	4/1934	11/1962(87F)	3/1961	1,465,365
5028	LLANTILIO CASTLE	5/1934	5/1960 (83D)	-	1,345,291
5029	NUNNEY CASTLE	5/1934	12/1963(88B)	-	1,523,415
5030	SHIRBURN CASTLE	5/1934	9/1962 (87G)	-	1,413,084
5031	TOTNES CASTLE	5/1934	10/1963 (84A)	5/1959	1,434,409
5032	USK CASTLE	5/1934	9/1962 (81A)	5/1959	1,288,968

DISPOSAL

5027	Cashmores, Great Bridge
5028	Swindon Works
5029	**Preserved**
5030	Hayes, Bridgend
5031	Cohens, Morriston
5032	Cashmores, Great Bridge

Castle class No 5025 CHIRK CASTLE is pictured 'on shed' at Oxford on 20 May 1961. *David Anderson*

Loco No 5025 entered GWR service in April 1934 and was allocated to Old Oak Common depot. BR shed allocations included Bristol Bath Road (82A), Oxford (81F) and Hereford (85C) from where the engine was withdrawn in November 1963.

Castle class loco No 5022 WIGMORE CASTLE is pictured moving 'off shed' at Wolverhampton Stafford Road on 31 August 1960. *Author's Collection*

Loco No 5022 entered GWR service in August 1932 and was first allocated to Old Oak Common depot; this locomotive was fitted with a four-row superheater and double chimney in 1959. BR shed allocations included Wolverhampton, Stafford Road (82A) from where the engine was withdrawn in June 1963.

A gala weekend at the Severn Valley Railway sees 1934 GWR-built Castle class No 5029 NUNNEY CASTLE powering towards Hampton Loade with a train for Bridgnorth. *Author*

Two enthusiasts sitting on the embankment enjoy the wonderful sight of 1950 BR-built Castle class No 7029 CLUN CASTLE (resplendent in pristine GWR livery) heading towards Chester on 8 March 1967. *Author*

GWR 1939-built Castle No 5080 DEFIANT heads across Berwyn Viaduct on the Llangollen Railway with a driver experience train. Master and pupil both look to be enjoying the occasion while smiling for the camera. *Author*

GWR 1936-built Castle No 5051 EARL BATHURST makes a fine sight and the clean powerful looks of Collett's design can be appreciated in this November 1992 study. *Author*

NO	NAME	DATE BUILT	WITHDRAWN	DOUBLE CHIMNEY	MILEAGE
5033	BROUGHTON CASTLE	5/1935	9/1962 (81E)	10/1960	1,160,197
5034	CORFE CASTLE	5/1935	9/1962 (81A)	-	1,250,714
5035	COITY CASTLE	5/1935	5/1962 (82C)	-	1,444,261
5036	LYONSHALL CASTLE	5/1935	9/1962 (81A)	12/1960	1,304,430
5037	MONMOUTH CASTLE	5/1935	3/1964 (82B)	-	1,500,851
5038	MORLAIS CASTLE	6/1935	9/1963 (81D)	-	1,438,862

DISPOSAL

5033	Cashmores, Great Bridge
5034	Cashmores, Great Bridge 5036.
5035	Cashmores, Newport
5036	Cashmores, Great Bridge
5037	Birds, Risca
5038	Cashmores, Newport

NO	NAME	DATE BUILT	WITHDRAWN	DOUBLE CHIMNEY	MILEAGE
5039	RHUDDLAN CASTLE	6/1935	6/1964 (81D)	-	1,380,564
5040	STOKESAY CASTLE	6/1935	10/1963(82B)	-	1,414,142
5041	TIVERTON CASTLE	7/1935	12/1963(81A)	-	1,383,804
5042	WINCHESTER CASTLE	7/1935	6/1965 (85B)	-	1,339,221
5043	BARBURY CASTLE	3/1936	12/1963(88B)	5/1958	1,400,817
5044	BEVERSTON CASTLE	3/1936	4/1962 (86C)	-	1,377,644

RENAMED LOCOMOTIVES

5043	EARL OF MOUNT EDGCUMBE 9/1937
5044	EARL OF DUNRAVEN 9/1937

DISPOSAL

5039	Cohens, Morriston
5040	Coopers Metals Ltd, Sharpness
5041	Cashmores, Great Bridge
5042	Birds, Bridgend
5043	**Preserved**
5044	Swindon Works

Preserved Castle class loco No 5051 EARL BATHURST
was originally named DRYSLLWYN CASTLE, and the
loco has on occasions carried that name in preservation.
The iconic Collett engine is pictured on Welsh Marches
Pullman duty in April 1983. *Author*

*After the return of preserved steam to the main lines of the UK
in 1971, the almost 140 miles long Welsh Marches route between
Chester and Newport saw a high concentration of steam-hauled
specials for the following 14 or so years. As 2010 dawned, the
picturesque route was still regarded as being steam friendly.
During the period some observers regarded as the halcyon years
for steam over 'the Marches', many types of locomotives were
used and they included regular performers King class No 6000
and Castle class engines No 4079, No 5051 and a rare visit by
Castle No 7029.*

Castle class No 5049 EARL OF PLYMOUTH is pictured arriving at Taunton station in 1958 with The Cornishman.
Author

Loco No 5049 entered GWR service in April 1936 and was originally named DENBIGH CASTLE; the loco was first allocated to Worcester depot. BR shed allocations included Cardiff Canton (86C) Newton Abbot (83A) and Bristol, Saint Philip's Marsh (82B) from where the engine was withdrawn in March 1963.

NO	NAME	DATE BUILT	WITHDRAWN	DOUBLE CHIMNEY	MILEAGE
5045	BRIDGWATER CASTLE	3/1936	9/1962 (84A)	1,383,737	
5046	CLIFFORD CASTLE	4/1936	9/1962(84B)	-	1,358,388
5047	COMPTON CASTLE	4/1936	9/1962 (84A)	-	1,225,670
5048	CRANBROOK CASTLE	4/1936	8/1962 (87F)	-	1,327,811
5049	DENBIGH CASTLE	4/1936	3/1963 (82B)	8/1959	1,282,965 *
5050	DEVIZES CASTLE	5/1936	8/1963 (82B)	-	1,135,797

*First of the class fitted with a four-row superheater 12/1963.

RENAMED LOCOMOTIVES		DISPOSAL
5045	EARL OF DUDLEY 8/1937	Cox & Danks, Oldbury
5046	EARL CAWDOR 8/1937	Swindon Works
5047	EARL OF DARTMOUTH 8/1937	Swindon Works
5048	EARL OF DEVON 8/1937	Hayes, Bridgend
5049	EARL OF PLYMOUTH 8/1937	Cashmores, Newport
5050	EARL OF ST GERMANS 8/1937	Coopers Metals, Sharpness

NO	NAME	DATE BUILT	WITHDRAWN	DOUBLE CHIMNEY	MILEAGE
5051	DRYSLLWYN CASTLE	5/1936	5/1963(87E)	-	1,316,659
5052	EASTNOR CASTLE	5/1936	9/1962(82B)	-	1,396,894
5053	BISHOP'S CASTLE	5/1936	7/1962(86C)	-	1,293,786
5054	LAMPHEY CASTLE	6/1936	10/1964(85B)	-	1,412,394
5055	LYDFORD CASTLE	6/1936	9/1964 (85B)	-	1,439,975
5056	OGMORE CASTLE	6/1936	11/1964(84B)	11/1960	1,434,833*

*Until December 1963 only thereafter (84B) became (2B) LMR.

RENAMED LOCOMOTIVES		DISPOSAL
5051	EARL BATHURST 8/1937	**Preserved**
5052	EARL OF RADNOR 7/1937	Cashmores, Newport
5053	EARL CAIRNS 8/1937	Cashmores, Newport
5054	EARL OF DUCIE 9/1937	Swindon Works
5055	EARL OF ELDON 8/1937	Cashmores, Newport
5056	EARL OF POWIS 9/1937	Cashmores, Great Bridge

Castle class No 5055 EARL OF ELDON is pictured 'on shed' at Newton Abbot on 24 May 1958. The loco has a full tender of coal and was in light steam when observed between two unidentified sister engines. *Colour-Rail/K Fairley*

Loco No 5055 entered GWR service in June 1936 and originally named LYDFORD CASTLE was first allocated to Old Oak Common depot. BR shed allocations included Old Oak Common (81A) Newton Abbot (83A) and Gloucester (85B) from where the loco was withdrawn October 1964.

Castle class No 5062 EARL
OF SHAFTSBURY is
pictured on the outskirts of
Bath, in September 1959.
Author's Collection

*Loco No 5062 entered GWR
service in June 1937 and
originally named TENBY
CASTLE was first allocated to
Wolverhampton, Stafford Road
depot. BR shed allocations
included Exeter (83C) Bristol,
Bath Road (82A) and Llanelly
(87F) from where the engine
was withdrawn in August 1962.*

NO	NAME	DATE BUILT	WITHDRAWN	DOUBLE CHIMNEY	MILEAGE
5057	PENRICE CASTLE	6/1936	3/1964(81A)	5/1958	1,273,324
5058	NEWPORT CASTLE	5/1937	3/1963(85B)	-	1,224,735
5059	POWIS CASTLE	5/1937	6/1962(84G)	-	1,054,602
5060	SARUM CASTLE	6/1937	4/1963(81A)	8/1961	1,316,240
5061	SUDELEY CASTLE	6/1937	9/1962(86G)	8/1958	1,020,412
5062	TENBY CASTLE	6/1937	8/1962(87F)	-	1,143,143
RENAMED LOCOMOTIVES			**DISPOSAL**		
5057	EARL WALDEGRAVE 10/1937		Swindon Works		
5058	EARL OF CLANCARTY 9/1937		Swindon Works		
5059	EARL OF ST. ALDWYN 10/1937		Swindon Works		
5060	EARL OF BERKELEY 10/1937		Cashmores, Newport		
5061	EARL OF BIRKENHEAD 10/1937		Cashmores, Newport		
5062	EARL OF SHAFTSBURY 11/1937		Hayes, Bridgend		

British Steam

NO	NAME	DATE BUILT	WITHDRAWN	DOUBLE CHIMNEY	MILEAGE
5063	THORNBURY CASTLE	6/1937	2/1965(84B)	-	Not known
5064	TRETOWER CASTLE	6/1937	9/1962(85B)	9/1958	1,155,986
5065	UPTON CASTLE	7/1937	1/1963(81A)	-	1,222,961
5066	WARDOUR CASTLE	7/1937	9/1962(81A)	4/1959	1,339,619
5067	ST FAGANS CASTLE	7/1937	7/1962(81D)	-	1,192,663
5068	BEVERSTON CASTLE	6/1938	9/1962(81F)	2/1961	1,081,514

RENAMED LOCOMOTIVES		DISPOSAL
5063	EARL BALDWIN 7/1937	Cashmores, Great Bridge
5064	BISHOP'S CASTLE 9/1937	Cashmores, Newport
5065	NEWPORT CASTLE 9/1937	King's, Norwich
5066	SIR FELIX POLE 4/1956	Cashmores, Great Bridge
5067	N/A	Cashmores, Newport
5068	N/A	Cashmores, Newport

Castle class No 5067 ST FAGANS CASTLE is pictured prior to departure from Bristol Temple Meads station in 1961; the driver is completing the regular pre-departure oiling procedure. Note that the engine is coupled to a Hawksworth tender, has BR pattern valve spindle covers but retains GWR-style tapered buffer barrels. *Colour-Rail*

Loco No 5067 entered GWR service in July 1937 and was first allocated Old Oak Common depot. BR allocations for this engine included Bristol, Bath Road (82A) Carmarthen (87G) and Reading (81D) from where the loco was withdrawn in July 1962.

Castle class No 5071 SPITFIRE is pictured passing Ealing Broadway on 2 September 1958 with a Cheltenham-Paddington express service.
Colour-Rail/D Ovenden

Loco No 5071 entered GWR service in June 1938 and originally named CLIFFORD CASTLE was first allocated to Newton Abbot depot. BR allocations for this engine included Newton Abbot (83A) Worcester (85A) and Bristol, St Philip's Marsh (82B) from where the loco was withdrawn in October 1963.

NO	NAME	DATE BUILT	WITHDRAWN	DOUBLE CHIMNEY	MILEAGE
5069	ISAMBARD KINGDOM BRUNEL	6/1938	2/1962 (83D)	12/1958	1,217,505
5070	SIR DANIEL GOOCH	6/1938	3/1964 (81A)	-	1,139,354
5071	CLIFFORD CASTLE	6/1938	10/1963(82B)	5/1959	1,150,913
5072	COMPTON CASTLE	6/1938	10/1962(84A)	-	1,055,942
5073	CRANBROOK CASTLE	7/1938	2/1964 (88B)	6/1959	955,495
5074	DENBIGH CASTLE	7/1938	5/1964 (82B)	9/1961	1,142,187

RENAMED LOCOMOTIVES		DISPOSAL	
5071	SPITFIRE 9/1940	Coopers Metals Ltd, Sharpness	
5072	HURRICANE 11/1940	Swindon Works	
5073	BLENHEIM 1/1941	Hayes, Bridgend	
5074	HAMPDEN 1/1941	Cashmores, Great Bridge	
5069	N/A	Swindon Works	
5070	N/A	Birds, Risca 5070	

NO	NAME	DATE BUILT	WITHDRAWN	DOUBLE CHIMNEY	MILEAGE
5075	DEVIZES CASTLE	8/1938	9/1962 (82B)	-	1,068,502
5076	DRYSLLWYN CASTLE	8/1938	9/1964 (81C)	-	1,121,080
5077	EASTNOR CASTLE	8/1938	7/1962 (87E)	-	1,089,166
5078	LAMPHEY CASTLE	5/1939	11/1962(87A)	12/1961	1,038,165
5079	LYDFORD CASTLE	5/1939	5/1960 (83A)	-	1,008,175
5080	OGMORE CASTLE	5/1939	4/1963 (87F)	-	1,117,030

RENAMED LOCOMOTIVES		DISPOSAL
5075	WELLINGTON 10/1940	Cashmores, Newport
5076	GLADIATOR 1/1941	Hayes, Bridgend
5077	FAIREY BATTLE 10/1940	Hayes, Bridgend
5078	BEAUFORT 1/1941	Swindon Works
5079	LYSANDER 11/1940	Swindon Works
5080	DEFIANT 1/1941	**Preserved**

Castle class No 5078 BEAUFORT is pictured at Paignton station with the 'Torbay Express' on 26 May 1958. *Colour-Rail/K Fairley*

Loco No 5078 entered GWR service in May 1939 and first named LAMPHEY CASTLE was allocated to Plymouth Laira depot. BR allocations for this engine included Newton Abbot (83A) Bristol, Bath Road (82A) and Neath (87A) from where the loco was withdrawn in November 1962.

Preserved Castle No 5080 DEFIANT is pictured approaching Ealing Broadway at speed with the Down 'Capitals United Express' on 2 September 1968.
Colour-Rail/D Ovenden

NO	STAR NUMBER	NAME	DATE BUILT	WITHDRAWN	DOUBLE CHIMNEY	MILEAGE
5081	-	PENRICE CASTLE	5/1939	10/1963(88B)	-	1,208,003
5082	-	POWIS CASTLE	6/1939	7/1962(81A)	-	1,161,413
5083	4063	BATH ABBEY S	6/1937	1/1959(85A)	-	1,001,686
5084	4064	READING ABBEY S	4/1937	7/1962(81A)	9/1958	1,188,386
5085	4065	EVESHAM ABBEY S	7/1939	2/1964(82B)	-	1,214,357
5086	4066	VISCOUNT HORNE S	12/1937	11/1958(85A)	-	1,060,724

S – Rebuilt Star class engines retained their names.

RENAMED LOCOMOTIVES		DISPOSAL
5081	LOCKHEED HUDSON 1/1941	Hayes, Bridgend
5082	SWORDFISH 1/1941	Cashmores, Great Bridge
5083	N/A	Swindon Works
5084	N/A	Cashmores, Newport
5086	N/A	Swindon Works

NO	STAR NUMBER	NAME	DATE BUILT	WITHDRAWN	DOUBLE CHIMNEY	MILEAGE
5087	4067	TINTERN ABBEY S	11/1940	8/1963 (87F)	-	1,088,932
5088	4068	LLANTHONY ABBEY S	2/1939	9/1962 (84A)	6/1958	1,047,102
5089	4069	WESTMINSTER ABBEY S	10/1939	11/1964(84B)	-	1,158,893*
5090	4070	NEATH ABBEY S	4/1939	5/1962 (81A)	-	1,161,961
5091	4071	CLEEVE ABBEY S	12/1938	10/1964(84E)	-	1,082,935*
5092	4072	TRESCO ABBEY S	4/1938	7/1963 (88B)	10/1961	1,143,594

*Up to 1963 thereafter (84B) became (2B) and (84F) became (2C) both LMR.
Rebuilt Star class engines retained their original names.

DISPOSAL

5087	Cohens, Morriston
5088	Swindon Works
5089	Cashmores, Great Bridge
5090	Cashmores, Newport
5091	Cashmores, Great Bridge
5092	Cashmores, Newport

Castle class loco No 5090 NEATH ABBEY is pictured arriving at Newton Abbot in June 1958. Note that the loco has a Hawksworth tender, BR-style parallel buffer barrels and valve spindle covers. *Author's Collection*

Loco No 5090 was rebuilt from Star class engine No 4070, entered GWR service in April 1939 being first allocated to Plymouth Laira depot. BR shed allocations for this engine included Bristol, Bath Road (82A) and Old Oak Common (81A) from where the loco was withdrawn in May 1962.

Castle class loco No 5098 CLIFFORD CASTLE is pictured over an inspection pit at Swindon on 24 September 1957. *Colour-Rail/K Fairley*

Loco No 5098 entered GWR service in May 1946 and was first allocated to Swansea Landore depot. BR shed allocations for this engine included Plymouth Laira (83D) and Wolverhampton Oxley (84B-2B after 1963) from where the loco was withdrawn in June 1964.

NO	NAME	DATE BUILT	WITHDRAWN	DOUBLE CHIMNEY	MILEAGE
5093	UPTON CASTLE	6/1939	9/1963(81A)	-	1,145,221
5094	TRETOWER CASTLE	6/1939	9/1962(82B)	6/1960	948,540
5095	BARBURY CASTLE	6/1939	8/1962(84G)	11/1958	1,122,493
5096	BRIDGWATER CASTLE	6/1939	6/1964(85A)	-	1,103,607
5097	SARUM CASTLE	7/1939	3/1963(88B)	7/1961	993,804
5098	CLIFFORD CASTLE	5/1946	6/1964(81D)	1/1959	826,525

DISPOSAL

5093	Swindon Works
5094	Cashmores, Newport
5095	Cox & Danks, Langley Green
5096	Cohens, Morriston
5097	Cashmores, Newport
5098	Cohens, Morriston

British Steam

NO	NAME	DATE BUILT	WITHDRAWN	DOUBLE CHIMNEY	MILEAGE
5099	COMPTON CASTLE	5/1946	2/1963(85B)	-	863,411
7000	VISCOUNT PORTAL	5/1946	12/1963(85A)	-	824,873
7001	DENBIGH CASTLE	5/1946	9/1963(84B)	9/1960	838,604
7002	DEVIZES CASTLE	6/1946	3/1964(85A)	7/1961	837,626
7003	ELMLEY CASTLE	6/1946	8/1964(85B)	6/1960	773,642
7004	EASTNOR CASTLE	6/1946	1/1964(81D)	2/1958	876,349

Renamed locomotive 7001 SIR JAMES MILNE 2/1948

DISPOSAL

5099	King's, Norwich
7000	Cashmores, Great Bridge
7001	Cohens, Morriston
7002	Cashmores, Great Bridge
7003	Cashmores, Newport
7004	Swindon Works

Castle class loco No 7000 **VISCOUNT PORTAL is pictured at Exeter St David's station with the Up 'Devonian' in July 1955.** *David Anderson*

Loco No 7000 entered GWR service in May 1946 and was first allocated to Newton Abbot depot. BR shed allocations for this engine included Newton Abbot (83A) and Worcester (85A) from where the loco was withdrawn in December 1963.

NO	NAME	DATE BUILT	WITHDRAWN	DOUBLE CHIMNEY	MILEAGE
7005	LAMPHEY CASTLE	6/1946	9/1964(85A)	-	869,370
7006	LYDFORD CASTLE	6/1946	12/1963(81A)	6/1960	789,052
7007	OGMORE CASTLE	7/1946	2/1963 (85A)	6/1961	851,649
7008	SWANSEA CASTLE	5/1948	9/1964 (81A)	6/1959	483,663*
7009	ATHELNEY CASTLE	5/1948	3/1963	-	671,920
7010	AVONDALE CASTLE	6/1948	3/1964	11/1960	669,192

RENAMED LOCOMOTIVES

7005   SIR EDWARD ELGAR 8/1957

7007   GREAT WESTERN 1/1948. Last express passenger engine built by the GWR.

*Up to 28 December 1963.

DISPOSAL

7005   Cohens, Morriston

7006   Birds, Risca

7007   Cashmores, Great Bridge

7008   Birds, Risca

7009   Cashmores, Newport

7010   Cashmores, Great Bridge

Castle class loco No 7006 LYDFORD CASTLE waits at Oxford with a Paddington-Worcester/Hereford train in May 1961. *David Anderson*

Loco No 7006 entered GWR service in June 1946 and was first allocated to Shrewsbury depot. BR allocations for this engine included Gloucester(85B) Plymouth Laira (83D) and Old Oak Common (81A) from where the loco was withdrawn in December 1963.

NO	NAME	DATE BUILT	WITHDRAWN	DOUBLE CHIMNEY	MILEAGE
7011	BANBURY CASTLE	6/1948	2/1965(84B)	-	716,784*
7012	BARRY CASTLE	6/1948	11/1964(84B)	-	667,408*
7013	BRISTOL CASTLE	7/1948	2/1965 (84E)	5/1958	1,898,571*
7014	CAERHAYS CASTLE	7/1948	2/1965 (84E)	3/1959	765,282*
7015	CARN BREA CASTLE	7/1948	4/1963 (81A)	6/1959	636,439
7016	CHESTER CASTLE	8/1948	11/1962(88B)	-	672,533

RENAMED LOCOMOTIVE

7013, renumbered 4082 and renamed WINDSOR CASTLE 2/1952 (locomotives identities swapped).

*7011 up to November 1962, 7012, 7013 and 7014 up to December 1963, (84B) became (2B) and (84E) became (2A) both depots LMR.

DISPOSAL

7011	Cashmores, Great Bridge
7012	Cashmores, Great Bridge
7013	Cox & Danks, Park Royal
7014	Cashmores, Great Bridge
7015	Coopers Metals Ltd, Sharpness then resold to Cashmores, Newport
7016	Hayes, Bridgend

Castle class loco No 7013 BRISTOL CASTLE which swapped identities with No 4082 is pictured having just backed on to its train at Paddington station in this 1960 image. Note that the fireman has retrieved the lamp from the rear of the tender and is walking forward with it. *Author's Collection*

Loco No 7013 entered British Railways service in July 1948 and was first allocated to Old Oak Common (81A). The identity swap took place in February 1952. BR shed allocations for this engine included Old Oak Common and Gloucester (85B) from where the loco was withdrawn in February 1965.

NO	NAME	DATE BUILT	WITHDRAWN	DOUBLE CHIMNEY	MILEAGE
7017	G.J. CHURCHWARD	8/1948	2/1963(81A)	-	724,589
7018	DRYSLLWYN CASTLE	5/1949	9/1963(81A)	4/1958	614,259
7019	FOWEY CASTLE	5/1949	2/1965(84B)	8/1958	680,454*
7020	GLOUCESTER CASTLE	5/1949	9/1964(81C)	2/1961	610,143
7021	HAVERFORDWEST CASTLE	6/1949	9/1963(81A)	11/1961	673,231
7022	HEREFORD CASTLE	6/1949	6/1965(85B)	12/1957	733,069
7018	DRYSLLWYN CASTLE	First Castle fitted with an experimental double chimney 5/1956			
DISPOSAL					
7017	King's, Norwich				
7018	Cashmores, Great Bridge				
7019	Cashmores, Great Bridge				
7020	Hayes, Bridgend				
7021	Cashmores, Great Bridge				
7022	Birds, Bridgend				

A very grimy looking Castle class No 7020 GLOUCESTER CASTLE is pictured at Didcot depot (81E) in May 1962 while receiving attention.
David Anderson

Loco No 7020 entered BR service in May 1949 and was first allocated to Old Oak Common depot (81A). Other BR shed allocations for this loco included Southall (81C) from where the engine was withdrawn in September 1963.

NO	NAME	DATE BUILT	WITHDRAWN	DOUBLE CHIMNEY	MILEAGE
7023	PENRICE CASTLE	6/1949	2/1965(84B)	5/1958	730,636*
7024	POWIS CASTLE	6/1949	2/1965(84B)	3/1959	731,344*
7025	SUDELEY CASTLE	8/1949	9/1964(85A)	-	685,916
7026	TENBY CASTLE	8/1949	10/1964(84E)	-	636,668*
7027	THORNBURY CASTLE	8/1949	12/1963(81D)	-	728,843
7028	CADBURY CASTLE	5/1950	12/1963(87F)	10/1961	624,626

*Up to 1963, (84B) became (2B) and (84E) became (2A) both LMR depots.

DISPOSAL

7023	Cashmores, Great Bridge
7024	Cashmores, Great Bridge
7025	Birds, Morriston
7026	Cashmores, Great Bridge
7027	**Preserved**
7028	Balborough Metals Ltd, Briton Ferry

NO	NAME	DATE BUILT	WITHDRAWN	DOUBLE CHIMNEY	MILEAGE
7029	CLUN CASTLE	5/1950	12/1965(85B)	10/1959	618,073
7030	CRANBROOK CASTLE	6/1950	2/1963 (81A)	7/1959	637,339
7031	CROMWELL'S CASTLE	6/1950	7/1963 (85A)	-	749,715
7032	DENBIGH CASTLE	6/1950	9/1964 (81A)	9/1960	666,374
7033	HARTLEBURY CASTLE	7/1950	1/1963 (81A)	6/1959	605,219
7034	INCE CASTLE	8/1950	6/1965 (85B)	12/1959	616,584

DISPOSAL

7029	**Preserved**
7030	King's, Norwich
7031	Cashmores, Great Bridge
7032	Birds, Risca
7033	Cashmores, Great Bridge
7034	Birds, Bridgend

NO	NAME	DATE BUILT	WITHDRAWN	DOUBLE CHIMNEY	MILEAGE
7035	OGMORE CASTLE	8/1950	6/1964(81A)	1/1960	580,346
7036	TAUNTON CASTLE	8/1950	9/1963(81A)	7/1959	617,653
7037	SWINDON	8/1950	3/1963(82C)	-	519,885

DISPOSAL

7035	Swindon Works
7036	Cashmores, Great Bridge
7037	Cashmores, Newport

GWR Collett Castle 4073 class locomotive No 7029 CLUN CASTLE is pictured at Foxhall Junction Didcot on 3 April 1965. *David Anderson*

The occasion was a 'Warwickshire Railway Society Great Western Steam Tour' to Swindon. The outward route was Birmingham Snow Hill-Banbury-High Wycombe-Greenford-Southall-Didcot-Swindon. While on the inward journey, the route used was Swindon-Oxford-Worcester Shrub Hill-Droitwich Spa-Bromsgrove-Barnt Green-Kings Norton where the Castle came off and was replaced by diesel loco No D5226 for the short final leg to Birmingham New Street.

PRESERVED CASTLE CLASS LOCOMOTIVES

Eight Great Western Railway Collett-designed '4073' Castle class locomotives have survived into preservation. In 2010 seven examples can rightly be described as being restored engines with the eighth still an incomplete kit of parts, on which some remedial restoration work has taken place. Of the restored engines three were in June 2010 listed as being on static display, two were in the workshops being rebuilt, pending a return to steam, and two examples operational and in fact passed for hauling trains on the main line. Six of the 'restored seven' have steamed for long periods in preservation.

4073 CAERPHILLY CASTLE

The first Castle to enter Great Western Railway service was loco No 4073 CAERPHILLY CASTLE on 31 August 1923. Introduced by Charles Benjamin Collett the new class of four-cylinder 4-6-0 express passenger type locomotives were in reality a development of Churchward's earlier and highly successful Star class, but with suitably increased dimensions. Newly completed loco No 4073 was exhibited at the British Empire Exhibition at Wembley in 1924 and the gleaming Swindon-built engine attracted a great deal of interest from not just the public but notably from officials of other railways.

Albeit an accepted development, and not a wholly new concept the Castle class proved to be extremely effective in service and can rightly be said to have influenced locomotive design/building well beyond the boundaries of the GWR. Following 'home and away' trials between Castle class engines and locomotives of Gresley design the London North Eastern Railway carried out modifications to some of their Pacific locomotives after taking into account the comparable performances of the GWR engines.

Furthermore the London Midland and Scottish Railway attempted to buy a batch of '4073' 4-6-0 locomotives from the GWR after borrowing one for use on the WCML, failing

Castle class leader No 4073 CAERPHILLY CASTLE is a National Collection engine and is pictured on display during 2009.

in that regard they went on to recruit from Swindon one Mr WA Stanier to their own staff! The aforementioned gentleman served at Swindon under both Churchward and Collett and it is impossible to deny the GWR influence in his later, and highly successful LMS designs.

Looking forward to the later introduction of the King class, while bearing in mind the Star/Castle development, locomotive design at the GWR has been described as being evolutionary in nature. Given the overall success of these three locomotive types, that would appear to be no bad thing! It is an acknowledged fact that steam locomotives even when manufactured in batches, and perhaps albeit by the same workforce could vary greatly in performance. Reportedly some Castle drivers could not wait to get a hand on the regulator of their rostered engine, while

on another day being given another engine they may have preferred a pannier tank!

Over 30 Castle class engines ran between 1.75 and two million miles individually in service, almost 100 clocked up totals of over one million miles per loco and 40 or so had recorded mileages of between 0.5 and 0.75 million miles each, with just one engine No 7037 SWINDON (the last built) only just topping the 0.5 million mile mark.

When withdrawn by British Railways from Cardiff Canton depot (89C) in April 1960 loco No 4073 had clocked up a remarkable 1,910,730 miles in service. Becoming part of the National Collection CAERPHILLY CASTLE was originally displayed at the Science Museum London but currently resides at Swindon Steam Railway Museum. To date there are no plans to restore this engine to working order.

Loco No 4079 is pictured in Didcot shed yards prior to the 1967 'Birkenhead Flyer Railtour'. *David Anderson*

4079 PENDENNIS CASTLE

No 4079 PENDENNIS CASTLE was outshopped from Swindon in February 1924 being the seventh of 171 Castles built. The loco served both her masters well running a recorded 1,758,398 miles in GWR and British Railways Western Region service. PENDENNIS CASTLE was employed during the 1925 locomotive trials alongside London & North Eastern Railway Pacifics and successfully worked 16 coach trains on the East Coast Main Line from London, King's Cross. Following the trials the GWR exhibited No 4079 alongside the LNER's famous FLYING SCOTSMAN at the 1925 British Empire Exhibition at Wembley with a placard proclaiming their engine to be 'the most powerful passenger express locomotive in Britain'.

After withdrawal by BR in 1964, PENDENNIS CASTLE was purchased for preservation by Mike Higson and appeared at one of the Great Western Society's first open days in 1965. The Castle was later bought by a partnership formed by the Honourable John Gretton and Bill McAlpine and was based at Didcot prior to the GWS establishing their Didcot Railway Centre

In 1977 the locomotive was sold again, this time to Hamersley Iron – one of the largest iron ore producers in Australia – for use on excursion trains on the company's 240-mile ore-carrying railway in the Pilbara region of Western Australia and No 4079 left England on 29 May 1977. In Australia, 'she' was looked after by the Pilbara Railways Historical Society, formed by Hamersley employees, and worked many excursion trains through the Chichester Ranges of Western Australia. A highlight of the Australian sojourn was a visit to Perth in 1989 to operate alongside her old rival FLYING SCOTSMAN as the climax of a tour during the country's bicentennial celebrations. However, vastly increasing traffic on the Hamersley railway introduced operational difficulties resulting in No 4079 being stored out of use for several

years, her final steaming in Australia took place in October 1994.

With prospects for an operational future in Australia looking uncertain, Hamersley Iron began to consider the options. The main concern was to find the loco a new home offering a secure future. It was also important that the engine should not become a stand-alone exhibit, but should play its part in illustrating the wider picture of GWR locomotive development. The decision to offer PENDENNIS CASTLE to the Great Western Society was made in the first days of 2000. In return, the society agreed to arrange and pay for the repatriation, and thereafter to restore the loco to full main-line running condition.

The locomotive was formally presented to the 'Society' by Hamersley Iron on 19 April. Following a 10-week voyage No 4079 finally regained British soil on 8 July 2000, 23 years, one month and eight days after she left. The cost of bringing the locomotive back to Britain had been met by generous donations from British enthusiasts aided by a grant from the Heritage Lottery Fund.

The locomotive's homeward sea route was via the Pacific Rim, the Panama Canal, the Eastern Seaboard of the USA and then across the Atlantic, the opposite way to her outward journey. The repatriation of No 4079 has been welcomed by steam enthusiasts many of whom who were deeply saddened when the engine left for Australia.

Restoration of the locomotive is currently under way at Didcot and the GWS welcomes offers of support. Comprehensive information concerning No 4079 has been collated by Drew Fermor for the Great Western Society, which can be accessed at www.didcotrailwaycentre.org.uk/locos/4079/4079.html. Alternatively contact: Richard Croucher, Great Western Society, Didcot Railway Centre, Didcot, Oxfordshire OX11 7NJ Tel: 01235 817200

Castle No 4079 PENDENNIS CASTLE is pictured hard at work under grey skies when passing Didcot North Junction, on 4 March 1967. The occasion being the Ian Allan sponsored 'Birkenhead Flyer Railtour'. The part of the route hauled by No 4079 was was Didcot-Didcot North Jct-Oxford-Banbury-Birmingham Snow Hill-Wolverhampton Low Level-Shrewsbury-Chester General and return. *David Anderson*

5029 NUNNEY CASTLE

After being withdrawn from service by BR at Cardiff East Dock in December 1963 No 5029 was delivered to Di Woodham's scrapyard at Barry Island in the spring of the following year. It languished at Barry for over 12 years where it was buffer to buffer with sister engine 5043 EARL OF MOUNT EDGCUMBE for a long period. In 1976 it was rescued and removed to The Great Western Society at Didcot, 'NUNNEY CASTLE' was the 81st loco to leave the scrapyard.

When originally purchased from Woodham's it was jointly owned by a private consortium and the Great Western Society. This arrangement changed in the mid 1990s when the loco became wholly privately owned. While it has recently changed owners, that remains the case to the present day. The loco was restored from scrapyard condition at Didcot and was returned to service in 1990. Since then it has been a regular performer on the main line and has visited several preserved railways.

In the late 1990s the engine was due for an overhaul and that work was carried out at Ian Riley's workshops in Bury, Lancashire. During this overhaul the loco was fitted with air braking (while still maintaining its vacuum system) and in addition the tender was modified to give a larger water capacity. Both of these modifications were made to enable it to widen its sphere of operation on the main

line. The loco subsequently returned to the main line in 2000 and in 2002 TPWS equipment was fitted.

In 2005 it was decided to inspect the loco and plan whether to perform an intermediate or full overhaul. In order to facilitate the inspections No 5029 was moved to Tyseley and thereafter it was decided to carry out a full heavy overhaul. To keep abreast of modern main line requirements the work included the fitting of OTMR equipment (locomotive black box recorder). On completion of the work the loco undertook a successful main line trial on 15 April 2008. Since then it has headed Vintage Trains excursions to Chester, York, Lincoln and Bristol and in addition has worked several 'Shakespeare Express' trains (see pages 58/59). It has also doubleheaded a tour with Tyseley classmate 5043 EARL OF MOUNT EDGCUMBE.

The loco is operated on behalf of its owner by a small group of enthusiasts, some of whom have more than 35 years' experience of preserved steam, and over 30 years of main line special operations. The 'Nunney Castle' crew are always willing to welcome anybody interested in assisting with the work of keeping the loco in running order. For more information about No 5029 visit website: www.5029nunneycastle.co.uk or email directly gwr5029@yahoo.co.uk

*Loco No 4079 entered GWR
service February 1924 and was
first allocated to Old Oak
Common depot. BR shed
allocations for this locomotive
included Gloucester (85B)
Bristol, Bath Road (82A) and
Bristol Saint Philip's Marsh
(82B) from where the engine
was withdrawn in May 1964.*

**Castle class loco No 5029
NUNNEY CASTLE is seen
with the Pembroke Coast
Express, passing Ferryside
en-route to Carmarthen on
12 January 2005.** *Author*

*Loco No 5029 entered GWR
service in May 1934 and was
first allocated to Old Oak
Common depot. BR shed
allocations for this loco included
Old Oak Common (81A)
Worcester (85A) and Cardiff East
Dock (88A formerly 88B) from
where the loco was withdrawn.*

5043 EARL OF MOUNT EDGCUMBE

Castle class loco No 5043 EARL OF MOUNT EDGCUMBE was outshopped from Swindon works at a cost of £4848 for the locomotive plus an additional £953 for the 4000-gallon tender. Originally No 5043 was given the name BARBURY CASTLE. It frequently hauled the GWR's 'Cheltenham Flyer', which was then the fastest train in the world. In 1937 No 5043 was renamed EARL OF MOUNT EDGCUMBE after a GWR Director.

Withdrawn in 1963 No 5043 was stored until the following spring when it was sold for scrap to Woodham Brothers' scrapyard at Barry Island, South Wales. That moved looked to herald the end of the line for 'The Earl'. However preservation came to the engine's rescue although at first in a round about way. In September 1973 the '7029 Clun Castle Limited' organisation purchased No 5043 to be a source of spare parts for their locomotive. As a result of which No 5043 was moved to Tyseley where many parts were removed for safekeeping and the locomotive 'hulk' stored awaiting its eventual demise.

In 1997 the 'Birmingham Railway Museum Trust' announced their ambitious project to restore GWR Castle EARL OF MOUNT EDGCUMBE to main line running condition. Specifications required that the locomotive should be in late 1950s condition with a Hawksworth tender and BR-style double chimney. The '5043 Restoration Fund' was set up to finance the work and loco No 5043 was thus finally reprieved from a death sentence!

Work to restore the loco started in 1998, the Friends of Birmingham Railway Museum (the former name for Vintage Trains Society) donated £10,000 towards the restoration of No 5043. The boiler was removed from the frames and prepared for inspection. Specialist welding work was completed on the boiler barrel by Babcock boiler specialists. That was the start of an almost 10-year labour of love for the Vintage Trains preservationists.

Meticulously restoring a main line express steam locomotive is a huge task and extremely costly in terms of not only money but also volunteer man hours. In 2008 amid great excitement No 5043 was exhibited in nearly complete form at the 'Tyseley 100 Open Weekend'. Following the event the final stages of assembly, painting and lining were undertaken.

On 3 October 2008, No 5043 returned to steam and moved under its own power again after almost 45 years! The restored engine returned to the main line on 16 October 2008, albeit a light engine move to nearby Shirley. On 19 October 2008, No 5043 made a loaded trip from Birmingham Snow Hill to Stratford but on the return trip it was removed from the train at Tyseley as the engineering staff were concerned about a warm axle box. This problem was attended to in time for 'The Earl' to appear in steam, and in action again as the star of the show at the '2008 Tyseley Open Day' and in time for its official public recommissioning on 26 October 2008.

The 'The Earl' is currently a regular performer on the main line and an ongoing special train career now beckons with trips already planned to Bristol along the western part of the 'Bristolian' route, along the Midland route to York, part of the West Coast mainline then the North Wales Coast to Llandudno Junction, the Welsh Marches route and the West Coast mainline from Crewe over Shap to Carlisle.

The Tyseley-based Vintage Trains preservationists believe that No 5043 will continue to be a prominent working example of the famous GWR Castle class in the future especially given its particular association with the 'Cheltenham Flyer', the 'Bristolian' and the legendary Old Oak Common motive power depot.

For more information visit www.tyseleylocoworks.co.uk/tlw/index.html

Castle class No 5043 EARL OF MOUNT EDGCUMBE is pictured passing Abergele & Pensarn signalbox on the North Wales Coast Route with the outward train of a Tyseley to Llandudno Junction round trip, 6 June 2009. Even in pouring rain the superbly turned-out '4073' class locomotive in full cry is a great sight to behold. *Pete Sherwood*

Castle class No 5043 seen at Tyseley as **EARL OF MOUNT EDGCUMBE** on 5 October 2008. *Brian Wilson*

Castle class No 5043 seen at Tyseley as **BARBURY CASTLE** on 26 October 2008. *Brian Wilson*

Loco No 5043 was originally built as BARBURY CASTLE and entered GWR service in March 1936 being then allocated to Old Oak Common depot. The engine was renamed September 1937, double chimney and four-row superheater fitted October 1958. BR shed allocations for this loco included Old Oak Common (81A) Cardiff Canton (86C) and Cardiff East Dock (88B later 88A) from where the loco was withdrawn in December 1963. No 5043 was bought for scrap by Woodham's, Barry in

5051 EARL BATHURST

Like the majority of the class No 5051 was named after a British castle which stood within GWR territory and that 1936 bestowed name was DRYSLLWYN CASTLE. However the loco only kept that title for some 15 months, being then renamed EARL BATHURST in August 1937; loco No 5051 has regularly carried both names in preservation. It is interesting to note that the name DRYSLLWYN CASTLE was used again by the GWR and on the second occasion was given to the 1938 built loco No 5076 but that loco also lost its Castle name, as in January 1941 No 5076 was renamed GLADIATOR as part of a batch of 12 Castles named after World War II aircraft types. In April 1949 BR built loco No 7018 was given the name DRYSLLWYN CASTLE.

No 5051 spent the greater part of its working life hauling trains from South Wales to London and the Midlands out of Landore (Swansea) depot and the engine was rarely seen elsewhere in service. Withdrawn by BR as surplus to requirements, from Llanelly depot (87F) in 1963, No 5051 was subsequently purchased for scrap by Woodham Bros of Barry.

The loco was rescued for preservation by a Great Western Society member, and brought to Didcot in February 1970. After ten years hard work the restored engine was outshopped in 1980 in time to take part in the Rocket 150 celebrations at Rainhill in May of that year. It then ran many main line specials (in the early years with Didcot's vintage train) until 1986 when the engine's first main line ticket expired. The loco was a regular and popular performer on the steam friendly 'Welsh Marches Route' during the period 1983/84 along with sister Castle No 4079 and King No 6000.

After the first preservation era boiler certificate ran out in 1990 the engine was overhauled for a second time and successfully returned to service once more gracing the main line, additionally numerous visits to other preserved railways and appearances in steam at, regularly, Didcot took place. In 2008 the latest boiler certificate expired and the locomotive was listed in 2010 as being on static display at the steam centre, and will remain so until such time as the third overhaul can take place.

For more information visit www.didcotrailwaycentre.org.uk/locos/5051/5051.html

Castle class No 5051 was a regular and popular performer on the steam-friendly 'Welsh Marches Route' during the period 1983/84. The loco is pictured while being serviced at Crewe Bank east of Shrewsbury on 9 April 1983. *Author*

5080 DEFIANT

No 5080 DEFIANT was one of the group of 12 Castle class engines which were named after World War II aeroplane types in 1941. The loco was originally named OGMORE CASTLE and as such entered GWR service in May 1938. The name OGMORE CASTLE was also used by the GWR on loco 5056 which in September 1937 became EARL OF POWIS, loco 7007 then carried the name until that loco became GREAT WESTERN in January 1948, with the name then passing to No 7035 in August 1950.

The loco worked extensively hauling main line express services which included the named trains the 'Red Dragon', 'Pembroke Coast Express' and 'South Wales Pullman'.

After being withdrawn by British Railways Western Region the engine was sold for scrap to Woodhams of Barry, where it languished for 11 years. No 5080 was purchased from the Barry scrap dealers along with two other GWR locos No 4160 a Collett built 2-6-2T and No 5637 a Collett-built 0-6-2T, the trio were purchased for the Birmingham Railway Museum at Tyseley (then the Standard Steam Gauge Trust) and left South Wales in August 1974. Initially the engine was acquired as a spare part donor loco for No 7029 CLUN CASTLE.

After a period of 11 years in store the restoration to main line standard of No 5080 began at the end of 1985 and an intensive work programme saw DEFIANT returned to working order on 11 June 1988. One of the restored engine's first tasks was to haul a train from Tyseley to Didcot while carrying the famous 'Red Dragon' headboard.

Above: **Castle class loco No 5080 DEFIANT is pictured during its 11-year sojourn at Woodham Brothers' scrapyard, Barry.** *Author*

Below: **No 5080 DEFIANT has been used on several railways as a 'Driver Experience' locomotive and is pictured while carrying out that role at Berwyn on the scenic Llangollen Railway.** *Author*

Since then, 5080 has visited numerous preserved railways including the Gloucestershire & Warwickshire Railway, Great Central Railway, Llangollen Railway and the Mid Hants Railway. 5080 Defiant was in 2010 on static display in the Oxford Rewley Road, ex LMS Station, which has been rebuilt at Buckinghamshire Railway Centre at Quainton.

For more information visit www.bucksrailcentre.org/index.php or www.tyseleylocoworks.co.uk/tlw/index.html

Loco No 5080 originally OGMORE CASTLE entered GWR service in May 1939 and was first allocated to Old Oak Common depot, renamed January 1941. BR shed allocations for this loco included Cardiff Canton (86C) Carmarthen (87G) and Llanelly (87F) from where the engine was withdrawn in April 1963.

7027 THORNBURY CASTLE

Loco No 7027 THORNBURY CASTLE is owned by the 'Waterman Railways Heritage Trust' and in 2010 is still very much a long term restoration project with some remedial work having been carried out, but the loco is basically in ex 'Barry' condition.

Loco No 7027 THORNBURY CASTLE entered British Railways (WR) service in August 1949 and was first allocated to Plymouth Laira depot. BR shed allocations for this engine included Plymouth Laira (83D), Old Oak Common (81A) and Reading from where the engine was withdrawn in December 1963. Sold for scrap to Woodham's, Barry in May 1964 No 7027 was eight years later purchased by the Birmingham Railway Museum and left as the 23rd departure from Barry in August 1972. The engine was later moved to LNWR Heritage Ltd at Crewe becoming part of the 'Waterman Railways Heritage Trust'.

Castle class No 7027 eases its Worcester/Hereford to Paddington train out of the platform at Oxford station in this 1960s image. Note the superb array of signals in the distance, also the fire shovel in the four foot (left foreground). *David Anderson*

7029 CLUN CASTLE

Loco No 7029 was constructed by BR at Swindon in May 1950 as one of the last batch of Castles (7028-7037). The preserved loco represents the final development of the Castle class incorporating all the modifications made in the 1950s. Outwardly, the only indication of enhanced performance is the double chimney, but internally the boiler has a four-row superheater and altered smokebox draughting arrangements. No 7029 was the last Castle to remain in BR service and was withdrawn in 1965.

On 9 May 1964 sister Castle class engine No 4079 PENDENNIS CASTLE was rostered to haul the 'Great Western' from Paddington on the first leg of the journey to Plymouth. The engine was expected to perform well on the prestige service but unfortunately the loco lost several faulty firebars in the vicinity of Westbury, and so was taken off the train. Standby engine No 7025 SUDELEY CASTLE was summoned and after a delay completed the journey to Plymouth.

The return service was rostered for loco No 7029 CLUN CASTLE and 'she' was more than equal to the task. The records show that as No 7029 neared the summit of Whiteball after the long climb (concluding with two miles at 1 in 115) 'she' still had enough steam in hand to lift the safety valves. The loco then thundered down Wellington Bank reaching 94mph before the driver had to brake to 80mph through Wellington station. Clear of the station precincts CLUN CASTLE accelerated again to an official 96mph, a speed some onboard observers clocked at 97mph! However No 7029 was denied the magic 'ton' with the 'Great Western' having to slow to 80mph because of the then governing speed restriction through Taunton station.

The engine continued to run superbly maintaining high speeds all the way to Bristol Temple Meads and arrived there 9¾ minutes early, to the great delight of several hundred welcoming enthusiasts. On that day CLUN CASTLE set the record (up to that date) for the fastest ever journey time by any form of traction, certainly between Taunton and Bristol, and other observers claimed possibly also between Exeter and Bristol.

The great performance had impressed a man with the strongest of railway connections, one John Trounson, a West Country mining engineer who was the fifth cousin to none other than steam pioneer Richard Trevithick. Mr Trounson who was a passenger on the train enlisted the help of fellow traveller Mr John Southern of Dodwalls Forest Railway fame and the pair subsequently started a 7029 preservation fund, which helped to kick-start the eventual purchase and preservation of CLUN CASTLE.

No one would deny that the 9 May 1964 Up run of the 'Great Western' was an outstanding feat and worthy of its place in the annals of steam locomotive achievements, however a few words of further explanation would be appropriate. Prior to the run CLUN CASTLE had been subjected to what could fairly be described as special attention by the Chief

Running Inspector for the Plymouth Division and his staff at Newton Abbot depot who had charge of the engine for three days prior to the off.

Inspector Cooke was very familiar with the loco and while he never claimed No 7029 to be the strongest Castle he had encountered he did believe that prepared properly, and driven in a certain manner 'she' would become what he reportedly described as a 'flying sewing machine'. During the days prior to the run every nut and bolt on the engine was double checked, all the lubricating gear was meticulously examined and new corks and worsted trimmings were fitted throughout. No chances were taken with the loco's ability to steam freely, accordingly the engine was steam tested!

Dawned the day and prior to the loco leaving the shed Inspector Cooke is reported to have personally given the handle of the oil pump several extra turns, to ensure that the oil was in all the right places. Thereafter he issued special instructions to the driver, including asking him to ensure that the loco be 'driven' at 18 per cent 'cut off' instead of the customary 15 per cent Castle setting. Driver Roach followed the inspector's instructions to the letter and CLUN CASTLE did indeed fly!

But what of the failed engine No 4079? PENDENNIS CASTLE was condemned immediately after the failure and left in a siding to await 'her' fate. Later however and fortunately before any BR paper work could catch up with 'her', a plan to rescue the loco was put together by Mr Michael Higson and others. The fact that No 4079 was marooned in the back of Westbury shed undoubtedly helped to secure her future for preservation.

A comprehensive account of No 7029's history and future prospects including an appeal to help fund the overhaul of the engine can be found at www.tyseleylocoworks.co.uk/tlw/7029.htm

Above: **Castle No 7029 CLUN CASTLE is pictured heading for Chester, on 4 March 1967. The occasion being the Ian Allan sponsored 'Zulu Railtour', ex London Paddington. The part of the route hauled by No 7029 was Banbury-Birmingham Snow Hill-Wolverhampton Low Level-Shrewsbury-Chester General for outward leg however on the return leg No 7029 came off the train at Wolverhampton Low Level where diesel traction was rostered to take over the train.** *Author*

Right: **CLUN CASTLE is pictured at Chester 7 October 1978 with the Pullman support coach usually associated with No 6000 KING GEORGE V. The picture was taken following a working of No 7029 from Hereford to Chester with 'The Fenman Railtour'. A Chester to Hereford trip on the same day ('The Marches Venturer') was rostered to be hauled by the King but due to a problem with that loco No 7029 operated the train.** *Author*

CLIVE HANLEY
CASTLE & KING SHOWCASE

Meet Warwickshire-based railway photographer Clive Hanley. "I was born in 1953 and brought up in West Lancashire at the time when steam was entering its twilight years; accordingly almost all the remaining steam locos were dirty black and mainly uncared for. From the grand age of 10 I enjoyed sneaky shed visits to Aintree, Edge Hill, Chester and even Crewe North (thank you to whoever placed that 45-gallon drum against the wall).

Without doubt however the highlights were several summer Saturday visits to Lostock Hall motive power depot, and I travelled there on a 2s 5d child return ticket from our family home in Maghull. With my elder brother and his mates I would bunk around the shed and then head over to the nearby WCML for a day's spotting, with of course our sandwiches and the obligatory bottle of Tizer!

A couple of indifferent pictures from that era were all that I could muster taken with a treasured 5s (25 new pence) plastic camera, which I purchased with the aid of a Kelloggs Corn Flakes offer! You could say that I'm now attempting to make up for all those missed opportunities.

My latest camera is the brilliant Nikon D700 (Digital SLR), coupled to a 24-70mm zoom lens. I also carry my old Nikon D50 coupled to a Nikon VR 70-200mm tele-zoom lens. For those rare occasions on loco footplates and where wide angle work is required I use a Sigma 12-24mm wide angle lens."

Enjoy Clive's latest collections online at:
www.clive-hanley.fotopic.net

Castle class No 5029 NUNNEY CASTLE commences the severe climb away from Tyseley Warwick Road station (within the Tyseley loco works) with 'The Lincoln Imp' railtour, 14 June 2008. *Clive Hanley*

Below: **Castle class locomotives No 5043 as EARL OF MOUNT EDGCUMBE and No 5029 NUNNEY CASTLE, seen at Tyseley Steam Open Day, 26 October 2008.** *Clive Hanley*

Castle No 5043 EARL OF MOUNT EDGCUMBE at a very rainy Leicester station with the returning 'Equinox Explorer' train, 19 March 2010. *Clive Hanley*

Three GWR Castle class locomotives at Tyseley. On the left loco No 5029 NUNNEY CASTLE, on the right No 7029 CLUN CASTLE and in the distance No 5043 EARL OF MOUNT EDGCUMBE (masquerading as BARBURY CASTLE), 26 October 2008. *Clive Hanley*

The 'King Circular' railtour of 17 March 2007, during which loco No 6024 KING EDWARD I is pictured at Didcot prior to joining its train. *Clive Hanley*

The 'King Circular' railtour of 17 March 2007, during which loco No 6024 KING EDWARD I is pictured at Didcot station. *Clive Hanley*

Three GWR Castle class locomotives at Tyseley. Left to right No 5043 EARL OF MOUNT EDGCUMBE (masquerading as BARBURY CASTLE) No 7029 CLUN CASTLE and No 5029 NUNNEY CASTLE, 26 October 2008. *Clive Hanley*

Castle class No 5043 EARL OF MOUNT EDGCUMBE heads along the single track section from Bearley towards Claverdon and about to pass Songar Crossing, 16 August 2009 with the 'Shakespeare Express'. *Clive Hanley*

KING OR SUPERCASTLE?

When the first King class four-cylinder 4-6-0 emerged from Swindon Works in 1927, it was not exactly met with universal acclaim. In fact, the unkindest critics immediately described the new express passenger locomotive class as being nothing more than a Supercastle! Be that unfair criticism or accurate assessment, our American cousins adopted a stance (as they would say) of 'makes no never mind anyhow'.

By all accounts, they loved loco No 6000 KING GEORGE V when that engine was shipped stateside to take part in the centenary celebrations of the Baltimore & Ohio Railroad Company. Before the ship carrying the loco had even docked on their side of the pond, a leader writer for the New York Herald Tribune had lyrically set the scene for his readers with a statement which could in modern terms be described as being perhaps just a little over the top!

"Breathes there a man with soul so dead that he doesn't thrill a little at such news? Especially when he learns that this engine, now under construction, will be capable of a speed of 80 miles an hour, the most powerful locomotive ever built for an *English railway". Possibly the American journalist had benefited from a degree of Swindon publicity office guidance? However, the locomotive did enjoy a great deal of success in the States and was credited with helping to attract over 1.25-million visitors to the event. * Perhaps with a little more thought he may have more correctly written 'a British railway'!

While in the USA, No 6000 impressed railway engineers by hauling with ease a 543-ton train from Washington DC to Philadelphia while attaining speeds up to 74mph. Meanwhile, at home, as the King locomotives went into service, questions were continually being asked, one in particular even rumbled on into the modern era. In the opinions of many observers, that big question has never been satisfactorily answered. Simplistically put, why were only 30 Kings built (1927 and 1930)? After all, Castles stayed in production until 1950. In the eyes of Swindon bosses, were the Kings perhaps not that much better a locomotive than their Castle cousins?

In this image taken at Wolverhampton Stafford Road depot on 10 November 1957, the wedge-shaped cab front associated with the streamlining of No 6014 KING HENRY VII can clearly be seen. Note also the hand-operated wiper on the front window, and also in comparison the conventional cab on loco No 6020 KING HENRY IV in the back ground. *Colour-Rail/K Fairey*

Loco No 6014 entered GWR service in May 1928 and was first allocated to Newton Abbot depot. BR allocated sheds for this loco included Old Oak Common (81A) and Wolverhampton, Stafford Road (84A) from where the engine was withdrawn September 1962.

King class No 6021 KING RICHARD II is pictured under those delightful signals at Didcott in 1961, on a 1.30pm Paddington-Bristol parcels. *David Anderson*

Loco No 6021 entered GWR service in June 1930 and was first allocated to Old Oak Common depot. BR shed allocations for this engine included Plymouth Laira (83D) and Old Oak Common (81A) from where the loco was withdrawn in September 1962.

Preserved National Collection loco No 6000 KING GEORGE V is pictured on the Craven Arms-Church Stretton-Shrewsbury leg of the Western Jubilee on 8 October 1977; the bell and cabside medallions presented to the locomotive during its American adventure in 1927 can clearly be seen. *Author*

The complete route of the steam-hauled excursion was London Paddington to Crewe and then return to London Euston. Diesel locomotives No 50004 and No 50005 were used on the first leg to Newport. Steam took over from Newport and SR Merchant Navy Pacific No 35028 CLAN LINE headed the first leg to Hereford. From Hereford to Craven Arms, LMS Princess Royal 4-6-2 No 6201 PRINCESS ELIZABETH took charge with the No 6000 then coming onto the train for the Craven Arms to Shrewsbury journey. Thereafter, LNER Gresley A4 No 4498 SIR NIGEL GRESLEY took the train on to Chester where first diesel and then electric traction (Crewe) took over to haul the train back to London. The special train was organised by the 6000 LA & MNLPS on behalf of the Steam Locomotive Operators' Association (SLOA) in order to celebrate the Silver Jubilee of H.M. Queen Elizabeth II.

Loco No 6000 entered GWR service in June 1927. The engine was shipped to America in August of that year to join in Baltimore & Ohio centenary celebrations. On return to the UK, the loco was allocated to Old Oak Common depot. BR allocations for this loco included Bristol, Bath Road (82A) and Old Oak Common (81A) from where No 6000 was withdrawn December 1962.

SIR FELIX POLE'S INFLUENCE

History suggests that the GWR supremo Sir Felix Pole was encouraged by certain board members, the most prominent of which in this regard being Sir Aubrey Brocklebank (a man whose opinions Pole reportedly had great respect for), to put pressure on Collett to produce a new more powerful express locomotive as a successor to the Castles.

Although proving highly successful in traffic, some in GWR engineering circles advanced the opinion that the Castle class design would have been an even better locomotive had a larger boiler been specified, and in fact use of the '4700' class boiler was an early consideration. Indeed, Churchward's idea for a more powerful Star class engine had earlier recognised the need for a larger capacity steam-raising unit.

However, low weight (axle loading) and therefore wide route availability was the prime mover in Castle construction, and therefore Collett included a smaller boiler in the design. The King class engines were built up to the maximum weight permitted on the GWR main lines at that time and consequently in service had severe route restrictions placed upon them.

The smoky confines of Wolverhampton Stafford Road loco shed. King No 6014 KING HENRY VII is pictured in the late 1950s. The King is in the company of Collett Hall 4-6-0 No 6901 ARLEY HALL. *Author*

POWER – THE BLUE RIBBON

In 1927, the Southern Railway Lord Nelson class had established itself in traffic and was heralded as the new 'most powerful locomotive class in Britain'. The tractive effort of the SR Maunsell four-cylinder 4-6-0 LN class was listed at 33510lbf as against the GWR Castle tractive effort of 31625lbf. The GWR took very personally the loss of that particular crown, and no one more so than Sir Felix Pole. The instructions to Collett were as wide reaching as they were simple: "the GWR must as soon as possible regain the title of operating Britain's most powerful express passenger locomotives!"

Starting at the end of the story is in this instance permissible, in explanation of the GWR favourable outcome. In June 1927, locomotive No 6000 KING GEORGE V met all the requirements; it and

the class which followed were indeed extremely powerful steam locomotives. The Southern Railway record was shattered as Collet's four-cylinder 4-6-0 King class design registered a phenomenal tractive effort of 40285lbf.

Simply put, tractive effort is a synonym of tractive force, and has traditionally been used in railway engineering to describe a locomotive's pulling power. In the steam railway formulae for calculating tractive effort, the resultant rating is derived from pressure, in pounds per square inch and lengths in inches, and is then shown as a given number of lbf's. As all UK railway steam locomotive builders used the same basic testing formulae and techniques, reference to a tractive effort comparison table of locomotives manufactured in the same time frame is appropriate.

King class No 6013 KING HENRY VIII is seen at Plymouth Laira depot (83D) in August 1958.
Colour-Rail/K Fairey

Loco No 6013 entered GWR service in May 1928 and was first allocated to Old Oak Common depot. BR allocations for this loco included Old Oak Common (81A) and Wolverhampton, Stafford Road (84A) from where the engine was withdrawn in June 1962.

TRACTIVE EFFORT COMPARISONS

COMPANY YEAR	LOCOMOTIVE CLASS	CONFIG	DRIVING WHEEL	CYLINDERS	BOILER PRESSURE	BR POWER RATING	TRACTIVE EFFORT
GWR 1 927/30	King 6000	4-6-0	6ft 6ins	4x16¼"x28"	250psi S/H	8P	40285 lbf
SR 1926/29	Lord Nelson	4-6-0	6ft 7ins	4x16½"x26"	220psi S/H	7P	33510 lbf
LMS 1927/30	Royal Scot	4-6-0	6ft 9ins	3x18"x26"	250psi S/H	7P	33150 lbf
GNR/LNER 1922/25	A3 Pacific	4-6-2	6ft 8ins	3x19"x26"	220psi S/H	7P	32910 lbf

THE KING CONCEPT

In the early 1930s, the King class engines answered their detractors well, consistently turning in excellent performances. Notably, the Kings regularly hauled 360-ton trains while maintaining tight schedules over the testing gradients of the GWR's West Country routes; on the same services, Castle class engines were limited to trains of some 415 tons. The introduction of Kings on the London-Plymouth route saw the 247-minute timing, which had existed for over 25 years, permanently shortened to 240 minutes.

The King class locomotives were considerably more powerful than the Castle class engines and in order to provide that power, the cylinders were increased from 16 inch diameter x 26" stroke (of the Castle class) to 16 ¼ diameter x 28" inch stroke which required a larger boiler, known as a Swindon 'Number 12' boiler. The Castle class locomotives built with a Swindon 'Number 8 'boiler had the same superheated working pressure as the Star class from which they evolved, i.e. 225psi. However, the King class working pressure was required to be 250psi, (superheated).

The low axle loading restraint which governed the Castle design (20 tons) did not apply to the heavier King class which had an axle loading of 22 tons 10cwt, initially restricting the use of the class to mainlines between London-Taunton and Plymouth, London-Bristol and London Birmingham-Wolverhampton. As the British Railways era came into being and permanent way improvements were put into

place, the Kings were additionally allowed on routes to South Wales through the Severn Tunnel and also between Bristol and Shrewsbury.

Churchwards Star class engines had driving wheels of 6 foot 8 ½ inch diameter; that dimension was also selected by Collett for his Castle class. However, for the King class, Collett reduced the driving wheel diameter to 6 foot 6 inches in order to gain more power. In another deviation from the Star/Castle design, the diameter of the King class front bogie wheels was reduced to 3 foot diameter (Castle/Star 3ft 2 inch). In overall length, the King class locomotives measured 68 foot 2 inches between buffers, and thus were 3 foot longer than the Castle class.

Because of the size, design and positioning of their cylinders, the King class locos required an entirely different design of front bogie. The resultant configuration was very much a GWR first in that the front bogie wheels were fitted with outside bearings while the rear bogie wheels had inside bearings, the end result being noticeably different even to the unpractised eye. King class engine No 6014 KING HENRY VII was the subject of a 'Bullet Nose' streamlining experiment in 1935 and gradually lost the embellishments over time until 1941, but retained a wedge-shaped cab. Over their life in GWR/BR service, the King class locomotives were extensively modified and also given new liveries on occasions.

King class No 6019 KING HENRY V is pictured leaving Didcot with a down express in 1956. *David Anderson*

Loco No 6019 entered GWR service in July 1928 and was first allocated to Wolverhampton, Stafford Road depot. BR allocations for this loco included Old Oak Common (81A) and Wolverhampton, Stafford Road (84A) from where the engine was withdrawn in September 1962.

King class locos required an entirely different design of front bogie. The resultant configuration was very much a GWR first in that the front bogie wheels were fitted with outside bearings while the rear bogie wheels had inside bearings, the end result being noticeably different. No 6024 is pictured on the turntable at Tyseley. *Brian Wilson*

BRITISH RAILWAYS KINGS

Modifications began by the GWR in 1947 when loco No 6022 KING EDWARD III was fitted with a four-row superheater and mechanical lubricator. Alterations introduced in 1948 by BR included locos 6009/6025 being given a new experimental livery of dark blue with red cream and grey lining. Modifications also included square edge steps to the top of the inside valve casings. All the class were gradually modified to receive four-row superheaters from 1949 onwards, following the successful trial of the method on loco No 6022.

In 1950, BR introduced a Standard Caledonian blue livery, with black and white lining, to the class. In 1952, and in order to improve draughting, 'sleeved' chimneys were fitted to locos 6001/6017, and additionally self-cleaning smoke boxes were introduced. The blue-liveried locomotives were gradually repainted in the more familiar and popular GWR Brunswick Green from 1952 onwards.

A controlled 'road test' in 1953 saw loco No 6001 KING EDWARD VII successfully haul a 25-coach train on a Reading-Stoke Gifford round trip, the loco having been fitted with modified larger diameter outside steam pipes. From 1954 onwards, cab roof ventilators became standard and locos were modified thus during their routine visits to the works. In the same year, use of the Alfloc water treatment regime was introduced on King class locomotives. The system, developed by British Railways in conjunction with Imperial Chemical Industries (ICI), was introduced in order to prolong boiler life by reducing the effects of corrosion and scaling.

In 1955, loco No 6000 KING GEORGE V was the first of the class to be fitted with a larger diameter single chimney; later locos 6003 KING GEORGE IV and No 6020 KING HENRY IV were similarly treated while No 6015 KING RICHARD III became the first of 14 locos of the class to be fitted with a fabricated double chimney and double blast pipe.

In 1956, the whole class was temporarily withdrawn from service in order to carry out front bogie repairs. On the BR Eastern Region, the Gresley streamlined 'W1' class loco No 60700 had suffered a derailment and a resultant enquiry had found that welded repairs to the front bogie of that loco had failed. A BR Western Region inspection prompted by those findings discovered that several King class engine bogies had developed fatigue cracks, and as a consequence reinforcing pieces were welded on all King bogie frame plates over time.

More outside influence of a North Eastern Railway origin appeared in 1956 when No 6004 KING GEORGE III became the first of the class to be fitted with a standard cast iron double chimney. That being a unit of NER design influenced by one RA Smeddle, who had joined the Swindon design team from Doncaster in 1951 with BR/WR man KJ Cooke (a former Hawksworth disciple) transferred in the opposite direction. No doubt devotees of both BR regions would claim with equal zeal that their man was the one sent 'abroad' on missionary work!

The NER-style cast double chimney truly altered not just the look of the King class but led to a marked improvement in performance. In fact, from 1956 onwards, the King class were effectively new engines as in turn they had also received new boilers, new inside cylinders and new front end framing, which was welded to the (retained) original rear section. In 1958, the self-cleaning smoke box configuration was replaced with a basket-type spark arrester which surrounded the double blast pipe.

The whole class was withdrawn in 1962, many railway observers believe prematurely, as the majority of the class were in excellent working order and the diesels replacing them were still unproven in traffic. In service, the Kings had proved to be reliable engines, relatively trouble free and capable of handling all the trains which were allocated to them. Drivers found them easy to handle and they rode well even at speed; moreover, skilful firemen were able to constantly maintain a plentiful supply of steam.

Last Collett GWR King in service for British Railways Western Region was loco No 6018 KING HENRY VI the engine is pictured on Didcot West Curve with the Stephenson Locomotive Society 'Farewell to the Kings' tour which took place on Sunday 28 April 1963. *David Anderson*

Loco No 6018 entered GWR service June 1928 and was first allocated to Plymouth Laira depot. BR allocations for this engine included Old Oak Common (81A) and Cardiff Canton (86C) from where the engine was withdrawn in December 1962.

King class No 6004 KING GEORGE III is pictured at Exeter, St Davids with a Plymouth-Exeter-Paddington express in 1956. *David Anderson.*

Loco No 6004 entered GWR service in July 1927 and was first allocated to Plymouth Laira depot. BR shed allocations for this loco included Wolverhampton, Stafford

GREAT WESTERN RAILWAY COLLETT KING 6000 CLASS DETAILS

Power Classification:	7P reclassified 8P by British Railways in 1951
GWR Power Class:	Special
GWR Axle Load code:	Double Red
Introduced:	1927-1930
Designer:	Charles Benjamin Collett
Builders:	Swindon Works GWR
Total Weight (working):	135 tons 14 cwt
Driving Wheel:	6 foot 6 inches
Leading Wheel:	3 foot 0 inches
Overall length:	68 foot 2 inches (over buffers)
Width:	8 foot 6 inches
Height:	13 foot 4¾ inches
Boiler Pressure:	250psi superheated
Boiler Type:	No 12
Fire Grate Area:	34.3 square feet
Cylinders:	Four 16 ¼ inch diameter x 28 inch stroke
Tractive Effort:	40,300lbf
Valve Gear:	Inside Walschaert with rocking shafts (piston valves)
Coal capacity:	6 tons
Water Capacity:	4000 gallons

30 engines built GWR/BRWR number series 6000 to 6029.

King class No 6027 KING RICHARD I is pictured at Exeter St Davids station in 1961. *Author's Collection*

Loco No 6027 entered GWR service in July 1930 and was first allocated to Old Oak Common depot. BR shed allocations for this loco included Plymouth Laira (83D) and Wolverhampton, Stafford Road (84A) from where the engine was withdrawn in September 1962.

Saturday 26 April 1975 saw 'KGV' haul the Hereford to Chester leg of the 'The Mayflower' special for Midland & Great Northern Joint Railway Society. No 6000 shared the haulage with Merchant Navy Pacific No 35028 CLAN LINE. *Author.*

Loco No 6000 was shipped to America in August 1927 to join in Baltimore & Ohio Railway Centenary celebrations. The 'engine' was presented with a bell and cabside medallions, which are still carried in preservation. The engine was allocated to Old Oak Common depot (81A) at the time of the formation of British Railways in 1948 and was withdrawn from that depot by BR in 1962. Thereafter leased to H.P. Bulmers Ltd, this marked the start of another 'working life', this time as a cherished preserved locomotive. 'KGV' is part of the National Collection of steam locomotives.

SUMMARY OF KING CLASS LOCOMOTIVES

The classic King design is seen to good effect as No 6004 KING GEORGE III prepares to depart from Exeter St Davids on an express for London Paddington. The driver has been busy with the oil can! *David Anderson*

Loco No 6004 was allocated to Plymouth Laira depot (83D) at the time of the formation of BR in 1948, and was withdrawn from Old Oak Common depot (81A). From the year 1920, Western Region locomotives carried cab-side identification markings in regard of their power and weight classification. The King class locomotives carried double red discs and a special power rating, confining them to only selected main line routes. The discs can clearly be seen on the cab-side of No 6004.

NO	NAME	DATE BUILT	WITHDRAWN	DOUBLE CHIMNEY	MILEAGE	REMARKS
6000	KING GEORGE V	6/1927	12/1962(81A)	12/1956	1,910,424	**Preserved**
6001	KING EDWARD VII	7/1927	9/1962(84A)	2/1956	1,941,044	Steam Trials
6002	KING WILLIAM IV	7/1927	9/1962(84A)	3/1956	1,891,952	
6003	KING GEORGE IV	7/1927	6/1962(86C)	4/1957	1,920,479	
6004	KING GEORGE III	7/1927	6/1962(86C)	11/1956	1,917,258	
6005	KING GEORGE II	7/1927	11/1962(81A)	7/1956	1,679,275	

Steam Trials. In 1953 Loco No 6001 was used by BR Western Region on special steam trials and while employed thus, hauled a 25-coach test train on a Reading to Stoke Gifford return trip.

DISPOSAL

6000	**Preserved**, originally leased to HP Bulmers Ltd, Hereford (Steam Centre)
6001	Cox & Danks Ltd, Oldbury
6002	Cox & Danks Ltd, Oldbury
6003	Swindon Works
6004	Swindon Works
6005	Cashmores Ltd. Great Bridge

Locomotive No 6006 KING GEORGE I is pictured at the once busy Plymouth Laira steam depot (83D) resting between turns in the shed yard during July 1961. Note that the loco has BR-style parallel barrel buffers and original valve spindle covers. *Author's Collection*

King No 6006 was allocated to Wolverhampton Stafford Road depot (84A) at the time of the formation of BR in 1948 and was withdrawn from that depot.

NO	NAME	DATE BUILT	WITHDRAWN	DOUBLE CHIMNEY	MILEAGE	REMARKS
6006	KING GEORGE I	2/1928	2/1962(84A)	6/1956	1,593,367	
6007	KING WILLIAM III	3/1928	9/1962(84A)	9/1956	1,437,609	Damaged
6008	KING JAMES II	3/1928	6/1962(84A)	7/1957	1,695,925	
6009	KING CHARLES II	3/1928	9/1962(81A)	5/1956	1,935,102	
6010	KING CHARLES I	4/1928	6/1962(81A)	3/1956	1,928,258	
6011	KING JAMES I	4/1928	12/1962(81A)	3/1956	1,718,295	

Damaged. On 15 January 1936 an express from Penzance collided with some coal wagons just outside the station limits at Shrivenham. The wagons were found to have become detached and 'run away' from an earlier train; tragically two people were killed and 10 others injured. Badly damaged locomotive No 6007 KING WILLIAM III was repaired, although many observers at the time described the post-accident engine as being a 'virtual rebuild'.

DISPOSAL	
6006	Swindon Works
6007	Cox & Danks Ltd, Oldbury
6008	Swindon Works
6009	Cashmores Ltd, Newport
6010	Swindon Works
6011	Swindon Works

NO	NAME	DATE BUILT	WITHDRAWN	DOUBLE CHIMNEY	MILEAGE	REMARKS
6012	KING EDWARD VI	4/1928	9/1962(84A)	2/1958	1,910,525	
6013	KING HENRY VIII	5/1928	6/1962(84A)	6/1956	1,950,462	Mileage
6014	KING HENRY VII	5/1928	9/1962(84A)	9/1957	1,830,386	Streamlined
6015	KING RICHARD III	6/1928	9/1962(84A)	9/1955	1,901,585	Chimney
6016	KING EDWARD V	6/1928	9/1962(84A)	1/1958	1,811,207	
6017	KING EDWARD IV	6/1928	7/1962(84A)	12/1955	1,853,262	

Mileage. Locomotive No 6013 had the highest recorded mileage in service of the class.

Streamlined. Locomotive No 6014 was fitted with 'Bullet Nose' streamlining from March 1935, which was removed by January 1943, except for the profile of the 'v'-shaped cab.

Chimney. Locomotive No 6015 was the first of the class to receive a double chimney.

DISPOSAL	
6012	Cox & Danks Ltd, Oldbury
6013	Swindon Works
6014	Cox & Danks Ltd, Oldbury
6015	Cox & Danks Ltd, Oldbury
6016	Cashmores Ltd, Newport
6017	Cox & Danks Ltd, Oldbury

Collett doubleheader! King No 6016 KING EDWARD V leads Castle No 5069 ISAMBARD KINGDOM BRUNEL, seen at Newton Abbot in 1959. Note that in this image the King still has original GWR tapering barrel buffers but modified valve spindle covers. Note that the then Laira based loco is minus a number on the smokebox door. *Author's Collection*

King No 6016 was allocated to Plymouth Laira depot (83D) at the time of the formation of BR in 1948, and was withdrawn from Wolverhampton Stafford Road depot (84A). Castle No 5069 was allocated to Old Oak Common depot (81A) at the time of the formation of BR, and was withdrawn from Plymouth Laira depot (83D).

Last Collett GWR King in service for British Railways Western Region was loco No 6018 KING HENRY VI; the engine is pictured at Steventon with the Stephenson Locomotive Society 'Farewell to the Kings' tour which took place on Sunday 28 April 1963. *David Anderson*

With reporting number 1Z77, the specially reinstated 'KING' made a return trip between Birmingham Snow Hill and Swindon Works. Outward journey Birmingham Snow Hill – Tyseley – Leamington Spa – Banbury – High Wycombe – Greenford – Southall – Didcot – Redbourne Lane – Swindon Works 'A Shop'. Inward Swindon Works – Swindon – Didcot North Junction – Oxford (water taken) – Banbury – Leamington Spa – Tyseley – Birmingham Snow Hill. The 34-year-old engine gave a good account of 'herself' attaining speeds in the region of 80mph during the trip with a fully loaded 12-coach train, a commendable achievement. King No 6018 was allocated to Newton Abbot depot (83A) at the time of the formation of BR in 1948, and was withdrawn from Old Oak Common depot (81A).

NO	NAME	DATE BUILT	WITHDRAWN	DOUBLE CHIMNEY	MILEAGE	REMARKS
6018	KING HENRY VI	6/1928	12/1962(81A)	3/1958	1,738,387	Last in service
6019	KING HENRY V	7/1928	9/1962(81A)	4/195	1,912,309	
6020	KING HENRY IV	5/1930	7/1962(84A)	8/1956	1,686,568	
6021	KING RICHARD II	6/1930	9/1962(81A)	3/1957	1,793,439	
6022	KING EDWARD III	6/1930	9/1962(84A)	5/1956	1,733,189	
6023	KING EDWARD II	6/1930	6/1962(86A)	6/1957	1,554,201	**Preserved**

Last in service. Locomotive No 6018 was designated last of the class in service by virtue of the fact that 'she' was reinstated by BR WR for a final King run on 28 April 1963. KING HENRY VI was officially withdrawn on 31 December 1962.

Preserved. Locomotive No 6023 was sent to Woodham Brothers, Barry, and subsequently rescued for preservation. Loco No 6023 had one pair of driving wheels severely damaged in a shunting incident. Was later sold to Brunel Trust, Bristol Temple Meads, and left South Wales as the 159th departure from Barry in December 1984. Preserved (now with new driving wheels) and is based at the Didcot Railway Centre.

DISPOSAL	
6018	Swindon Works
6019	Cashmores Ltd, Newport
6020	Cox & Danks, Oldbury
6021	Cashmores Ltd, Newport
6022	Cox & Danks Ltd, Olbury
6023	**Preserved**

British Steam

NO	NAME	DATE BUILT	WITHDRAWN	DOUBLE CHIMNEY	MILEAGE	REMARKS
6024	KING EDWARD I	6/1930	6/1962(86C)	3/1957	1,570,015	**Preserved**
6025	KING HENRY III	7/1930	12/1962(81A)	3/1957	1,836,713	
6026	KING JOHN	7/1930	9/1962(81A)	3/1958	1,622,350	
6027	KING RICHARD I	7/1930	9/1962(84A)	8/1956	1,836,535	
6028	KING GEORGE VI	7/1930	11/1962(81A)	1/1957	1,663,271	Renamed
6029	KING EDWARD VIII	8/1930	7/1962(81A)	12/1957	1,859,278	Renamed

Preserved. Locomotive No 6024 was sent to Woodham Brothers, Barry, and subsequently rescued for preservation. KING EDWARD I was sold to restorers at Quainton Road, and left as the 36th departure from Barry in March 1973, currently owned, preserved and operated by the '6024 Preservation Society'.

Renamed. Locomotive No 6028 was originally named KING HENRY II and was renamed in January 1937; while loco No 6029, which originally carried the name KING STEPHEN, and was renamed in May 1936.

DISPOSAL

6024	**Preserved**
6025	Swindon Works
6026	Swindon Works
6027	Cox & Danks Ltd, Oldbury
6028	Birds Ltd, Risca
6029	Cashmores Ltd

Loco No 6026 KING JOHN is pictured at Exeter St. Davids station in 1960. Note the fireman about his duties on the top of the tender. *Author's Collection*

King No 6026 was allocated to Old Oak Common depot (81A) at the time of the formation of BR in 1948, and was withdrawn from that depot.

Fresh from Swindon Works after overhaul, King No 6009 KING CHARLES II heads out of Didcot station with an early afternoon two-coach all stations local stopping train to Swindon (running in turn) on 13 May 1961, serving stations at Steventon, Wantage Road, Challow and Shrivenham. This local service was regularly used as a running in turn before ex works locos were returned to their home depot, in this case Old Oak Common (81A). *David Anderson*

Loco No 6009 entered GWR service in March 1928. The locomotive's first and last shed allocation was Old Oak Common from where the engine was withdrawn in September 1962.

PRESERVED KING CLASS LOCOMOTIVES

Three Collett-designed four-cylinder 4-6-0 King '6000' class locomotives survived into preservation. Two were rescued from Woodham Brothers, Barry, South Wales scrapyard but importantly the class leader locomotive No 6000 was sold directly into preservation and in 1971 became the first steam locomotive to break the British Railways main line steam ban, which had been in place since 1969. In 2010 one King class engine is listed as being on static display while another is available for main line service and the third nearing the end of an understandably protracted restoration effort.

6000 KING GEORGE V

This locomotive is arguably the most famous ex Great Western Railway preserved engine and is a part of the national collection of steam locomotives. Currently with its boiler 'out of ticket' and being in need of a complete overhaul the King class leader in the spring of 2010 was listed as being on static display in the Great Hall of the National Railway Museum at York.

Loco No 6000 could possibly be moved to another location in the near future as a huge refurbishment project is planned to take place at the NRM.

When withdrawn from BR service in December 1962 loco No 6000 had recorded 1,910,424 miles in service for the GWR and BR Western Region. The rescued locomotive went first to the then Bulmer's Railway Centre at Hereford and after being overhauled became the steam locomotive which led the preservation era 'return to steam' on British Railways tracks. As such the engine became well known among both enthusiasts and members of the public.

The historic engine still carries the commemorative bell and cabside medallions which were presented during the 1927 visit to the Baltimore & Ohio Railway Centenary celebrations in the United States of America. While currently displayed loco No 6000 is dimensionally 'as built' and effectively in final BR/WR condition. To facilitate running on the present day railway network preserved King class No 6024 has had the original chimney, safety valve bonnet and cab cut down to allow for the reduced clearance under bridges, resulting from modern deeper ballasting regimes. Carrying out this work to No 6000 is considered unnecessary for the present time due to the availability in service of the other preserved King class engines.

Top: **The clean powerful looking lines of King class No 6000 KING GEORGE V are seen to good effect in this preservation era image of the loco.** *Author*

No 6000 left Swindon Works in June 1927 and was shipped to America in August of that year in order to join in Baltimore & Ohio Railway Centenary celebrations. On its return to the UK the engine was allocated to Old Oak Common depot. BR shed allocations included Bristol, Bath Road (82A) and Old Oak Common (81A) from where the engine was withdrawn.

6023 KING EDWARD II

The rescue and subsequent restoration to main line standard of loco No 6023 when compared to the other two rescued King class engines may well be seen by the casual observer as being a rather protracted affair, but perhaps the achievement should be more accurately described (after its pending completion) as a real mission impossible! Withdrawn by BR in June 1962 KING EDWARD II was bought by Woodham Brothers in December of that year, moved to Barry and there left to the mercy of the South Wales sea air for over 20 years.

Rescue came for No 6023 in December 1984 when the engine, which was by then virtually a rotting hulk, finally left Barry as the 159th departure from that famous elephant's graveyard. But not before the once noble King had suffered the ignominy of having the rear driving wheel set sliced through with a cutter's torch, following a shunting accident and derailment at the site. To add insult to injury the engine was over time stripped of many component parts, some of which were taken away to be used on other restoration projects.

A great many steam locomotive enthusiasts made the pilgrimage to Barry Docks and in the main were allowed by the redoubtable late Di Woodham and his staff to pay homage to the redundant steamers. Others of a more involved persuasion even commenced restoration projects at the scrapyard hoping that one day 'their engine' would be repatriated. Not all of those projects came to fruition but fortunately the large majority did. This writer recalls making such Barry visits and particularly during a November 1971 being greatly saddened by the sight of loco No 6023 standing forlornly, complete with the crippled rear driving wheel set!

The initial rescue of loco 6023 KING EDWARD II was made possible by the efforts of the Brunel Trust, Temple Meads, who moved the engine to that city. There the long slow process of restoring loco No 6023 to working order work got under way and continued until the autumn of 1988 when the funding for the initial restoration work was discontinued. Not only did the work then cease but unfortunately some parts which had been sent away for contract work to be carried out (cab sides, tender tanks etc) were then reportedly scrapped when it became known that payment for that work might not be made available. Effectively the worthy restoration of KING EDWARD II hit the buffers!

As news of the problem spread around the preservation movement others became determined to take over the preservation of Collett King class No 6023, most notably the Great Western Society (GWS). Early in 1989 a deal was agreed and to facilitate the return to steam of loco 6023 the GWS bought the engine for a sum in the region of £16K. The locomotive was then reduced to component parts, boiler, frames, wheels and tender etc and in March 1990 was moved, by train, from Bristol to Didcot.

The first big problem for those involved with the project was making good the rear driving wheels and to that end a magnificent wooden pattern was made up for the castings. The loco was subsequently re-wheeled on 1 July 1995, exactly 65 years after being put into service by the GWR. Work then progressed gradually on the manufacture of new motion gear, four connecting rods, three coupling rods, two eccentric rods, four crossheads, four piston rods and 10 suspension springs. Additionally all the surviving rods were refurbished.

Loco No 6023 is pictured at Barry in November 1971 and in this image the 'cut' damage rear driving wheel set can be clearly be seen. *Author*

For a period 6023 was turned out by BR in blue, and it is intended that 6023 will appear in this guise again. The under restoration engine is pictured on the turntable at Didcot in May 2010. The tender is painted in a BR 'Oxford Blue' finishing coat and the loco as pictured is still in undercoat showing a colour which is close to the 'Caledonian Blue' which for a while some King class engines carried. The GWS say that the completed locomotive will initially carry the 'Oxford Blue' livery.
Phil Neale

Loco No 6023 entered GWR service in June 1930 and was first allocated to Newton Abbot depot. BR allocations for this loco included Plymouth Laira (83D) and Old Oak Common (81A) from where the engine was withdrawn in June 1962.

As rescued loco 6023 was in double chimney form but one of the aims of the project is to produce a 'single chimney King' as it was in its original guise. In 1997 a single chimney and blastpipe arrangement was reunited with the smokebox. The most time-consuming aspect of the project has been the manufacture and/or refurbishment of hundreds of items such as steel cladding for the boiler, handles, levers, a huge amount of piping of various bores, hangers, steel flooring, buffers, nuts, bolts and various steam and vacuum valves, injectors and ejectors. The locomotive's tender has been restored as a separate project at the Severn Valley Railway and LNWR Heritage Ltd Crewe.

After the manufacturing and fitting of the valve gear was completed, work progressed through 2005-6 on the complex job of setting the valves, which required the engine motion to be painstakingly turned by hand. To allow this

the newly made rear wheels were disconnected from the rest of the motion by removing the rear connecting rods, and the setting up of sets of rollers under the front and middle sets of wheels. Using an air-driven pump and a person turning each roller (with a 6ft long ratchet) the wheels were rotated slowly so that measurements and adjustments to the valve timing could be made.

The firebox and retubed boiler has been completed and a new ash pan fabricated, additionally the mechanical lubricator pipes have been installed and a myriad other jobs completed. With cladding in place loco No 6023 is now beginning to look the part. The restoration is now on the final lap but is still dependent on donations. If you wish to support this project with a donation, please contact www.6023.co.uk/ or www.didcotrailwaycentre.org.uk/guide/projects.html

6024 KING EDWARD I

Withdrawn from BR service in the June of 1962 King class loco No 6024 was bought for scrap by Woodham Brothers of Barry, South Wales. There KING EDWARD I languished in the company of over 200 other locomotives, while fortunately the scrap merchants' cutting torches were applied to easier and possibly more lucrative targets.

King class leader loco No 6000 had made an impressive return to the main line in 1971 and inspired by that successful venture the 1973-formed King Preservation Society raised a sum in the region of £4K in order to buy engine No 6024 KING EDWARD I to ensure that another Collett King was saved for preservation. A reasonable sum when you consider that 11 years later No 6023 attracted a scrap price of three times that amount. Interestingly the 'mixed scrap metal' going rate for a steam locomotive at the time BR disposed of their fleet was approximately £10 a ton. Therefore a King class loco and tender with a combined (empty) weight of 104 tons would have had a basic scrap value of £1040.

Of the two King class locomotives at Barry No 6024, although with slide bars, piston rods, connecting and eccentric rods cut through, was considered to be the better purchase option.

Leaving Barry as the 36th rescued steam locomotive No 6024 was moved to the Buckinghamshire Railway Centre at Quainton Road where the slow and exacting process of restoring the engine to main line standard got under way. That process was to become a 16-year long labour of love, for the first 12 years of which the loco remained in the open air. On the 2 February 1989 loco No 6024 moved again under its own power and on 26 April 1989 KING EDWARD I (affectionately known as Spud 1) was recommissioned by HRH the Duke of Gloucester.

Above: **Loco No 6024 KING EDWARD 1 is pictured in the 'condemned line' at Woodham Brothers scrapyard Barry, South Wales, in November 1971.** *Author*

Left: **No 6024 and support coach pictured at Tyseley Locomotive Works on 3 October 2004.** *Brian Wilson*

Loco No 6024 entered GWR service in June 1930 and was first allocated to Plymouth Laira depot. BR shed allocations included Old Oak Common (81A) and Cardiff Canton (88A formally 86C) from where the engine was withdrawn in June 1962 after 32 years in GWR/BR service.

No 6024 at the Severn Valley Railway on 15 November 2009. The loco was working the Sunday Diner and that was the only train worked by 6024 during that visit to the SVR. *Fred Kerr*

To complete the engine's return to main line standard it was then moved to Tyseley Locomotive Works (then Birmingham Railway Museum) from where test runs were carried out before 'Spud 1' successfully embarked upon a second career as a restored main line certificated King class locomotive. In recognition of the high standard to which the locomotive had been restored, No 6024 was outright winner of the 1990 British Coal sponsored Heritage Award (for a restoration project using coal), and was awarded a prize of £3K, which was used to help restore a Mark I BSK coach for transporting support crew and equipment during main line work.

After successfully hauling charter trains to all parts of the UK rail network No 6024 was rostered to haul the Intercity VIP Special on 19 May 1990 and later (during an event to celebrate 60 years of Swindon Works) the loco was displayed alongside sister engine No 6000. After being fitted with BR's Automatic Warning System (permitting speeds up to 75mph), No 6024 was active on trains to a number of destinations within western zones, those charters included steam-hauled trains to Cardiff, Bristol Temple Meads, Gloucester, Exeter, Swansea, Worcester, Newton Abbot and Paignton after an absence of many years.

By early 1995 the loco had run almost 10,000 miles in preservation (following 1.57 million miles in GWR/ BR service) and accordingly was withdrawn from traffic in March 1995 to facilitate a heavy overhaul and following the expiration of its boiler certificate. The loco emerged from the MOD Kineton site in September 1996 on the completion of that work and also after having been modified in order to make the loco more suited to the prevailing network conditions.

Those modifications included the fitting of dual-braking equipment (air and vacuum) additionally the reduction of its chimney, safety valves and cab-roof heights. Thereafter the loco made first a double headed, and then a solo trip to Plymouth in 1997. In August 2002 with the 'Eden Express' for Pathfinder Tours KING EDWARD I set a new record for steam with the fastest preservation era recorded time over the 52 miles from Plymouth to Exeter, in a time of 58 minutes 6 seconds.

In October 2002 the locomotive was withdrawn from traffic for its second major overhaul having clocked up a further 15,000 miles. On that occasion the work was carried out by the Society at Tyseley Locomotive Works. To keep pace with safety improvements the locomotive was also fitted with standard Train Protection Warning System (TPWS), and notably the Society also completed its Water Wagon project for main line trials. That enabled main line water-stops to be avoided on certain routes.

King class loco No 6024 subsequently returned to the main line on 7 October 2004, with its third seven-year main line certificate.

During the busy main line schedules which followed No 6024 passed a major milestone when on 2 July 2005 KING EDWARD I celebrated its 75 anniversary, by hauling a special train from Paddington to Kingswear. During subsequent maintenance work at Tyseley No 6024 was fitted with the so called 'Black Box' equipment, for on-train data monitoring and recording (OTMR).

The first charter train run utilising the aforementioned water-wagon took place in June 2007, between Shrewsbury and Paddington, a distance of 170 miles during which, as anticipated, no water-stops were required. The year 2010 marks the 80th anniversary of 6024's entry into service with the Great Western Railway, in July 1930. For more information about loco No 6024 and the locomotive's owning society visit www.6024.com

GWR STREAMLINERS

In order not to be completely outdone by the other railway companies and in line with the 1930s fascination with steam locomotive streamlining the Great Western board of directors instructed Collett to design suitable embellishments for Castle and King class locomotives. The resultant 1935 design could at best only be described as being semi-streamlined, and perhaps not overly imaginative. Reportedly the basic scheme resulted from Plasticine smoothing being applied to a model of the King class by Collett's design team.

While other railway companies had whole classes of streamlined/air smoothed casing express passenger locomotives the GWR opted to have only two steam streamliners. Many observers at the time commented that the best thing about the GWR embellishments was the fact that only two were put into service! Unkind comments perhaps but it is hard to deny that the design changes, done in the name of fashionable refinement, completely spoiled the look of the previously handsome Collett four-cylinder 4-6-0s. The engines chosen for the GWR experiment were King No 6014 KING HENRY VII and Castle No 5005 MANORBIER CASTLE, accordingly the two re-entered traffic complete with their streamlined embellishments in March 1935.

The most striking (some may say incongruous) feature of the Swindon streamlined design was the bullet nose fitted to the smokebox of each engine. Other modifications included fairings behind the locos' chimneys and safety valve casings. Curved spectacle plates were added to the front of the cabs and additionally an extension piece fabricated which aligned the top of the tender with a cab roof extension. Both locomotives were given 'V' fronted cabs and plating was added to their front ends in order to aid air smoothing.

The air smooth casings at the front end of the locos caused problems in service namely with overheating and restricted accessibility. Importantly the Castle class engines utilised a system of condensing steam and oil in order to provide lubrication for the inside cylinder valve guides. The fairings had the effect of reducing the amount of oil condensed to such a low level that it became ineffective as a lubricant, simply put the deposit of oil on the slide bars was so small that it effectively dried out. Measures subsequently taken to rectify this problem included replacing the usual two-feed oil boxes with repositioned four-feed units.

However the streamlining was not destined to be long lasting in service and by the end of 1935 the front end air smoothing and cab roof extensions had been removed from both engines. There was piecemeal removal of embellishments between 1939 and 1945 and by 1947 the streamlining was gone; loco No 5005 MANORBIER CASTLE received a new normal square front end cab in that year but the 'V' cab applied to No 6014 KING HENRY VII remained with the engine for the rest of its working life.

The fascinating selection of images and drawings has been provided by the Great Western Society (GWS). The GWS has preserved a wide ranging collection of items at Didcot Railway Centre from the Great Western Railway covering the evolution of railways over 125 years through the history of one company – the GWR; 2010 marks the 175th anniversary of the creation of the Great Western Railway. For more information visit: http://www.didcotrailwaycentre.org.uk/getting_involved/membership.html
All images Great Western Society

Opposite top: **Castle class 4-6-0 No 5005 MANORBIER CASTLE. The loco is seen at speed in this 1936 image. Note that the cab extension and tender plating is still in place.**

Opposite right: **King class 4-6-0 No 6014 KING HENRY VII. This is the official 1935 Swindon Works picture of No 6014. One can only imagine the comments of the travelling public!**

Below: **King class 4-6-0 No 6014 KING HENRY VII. The loco is seen in traffic in this 1935 image. Note the signal the photographer is fortunate not to have been 'blanked' by a train travelling the other way.**

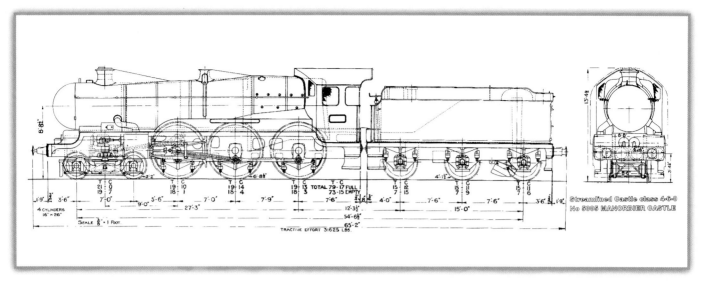

Streamlined Castle class 4-6-0
No 5005 MANORBIER CASTLE

Castle class 4-6-0 No 5005 MANORBIER CASTLE. In this 1935 image the GWR official is showing the location of a front inspection cover.

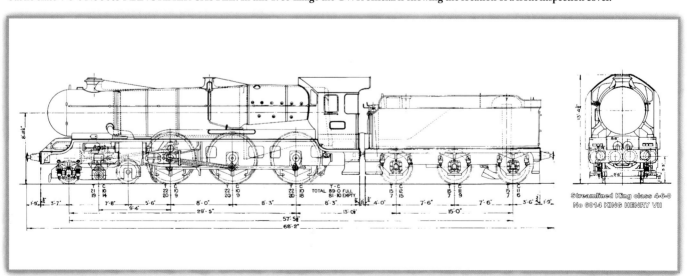

Streamlined King class 4-6-0
No 6014 KING HENRY VII

DAVID ANDERSON SHOWCASE
BR/WR CASTLE & KING LOCOMOTIVES

British Railways took into stock 30 Collett 4-6-0 '6000' King class four-cylinder locomotives and 151 Collett 4-6-0 '4073' Castle class four-cylinder locomotives on.1 January 1948. That organisation then built a further 20 Castle class engines in 1950 thus bringing the Castle built total to 171. However BR never had more than 170 in service at any one time as rebuilt Star class Castle loco No 100 A1 LLOYD'S was withdrawn in March 1950 almost six months before the last Castle loco No 7037 SWINDON entered service.

Castle class engines did not see dramatic reductions in their number until 1962 when by the end of that year only 93 remained in service; that number was almost halved by the end of 1963 when only 49 Castle class engines were listed as serviceable. Only 12 class members made it beyond the end of 1964, the last of the class to be withdrawn being the now preserved loco No 7029 CLUN CASTLE, withdrawn in December 1965.

The official deadline for steam operation on BR/WR was in fact September 1965. However the Western Region had an initial shortage of diesel engines with which to work the London Paddington-Worcester express services. To solve the temporary

traction shortage Worcester-based steam locos which had already been sold for scrap and laid aside were leased back by BR/WR at a reported cost of £100 per week, perchance the first examples of privately owned engines working on British Railways?

No individual King class engines were withdrawn by BR between 1948 and the official end of their use in 1962, however loco No 6018 KING HENRY VI was withdrawn in September 1962 and then temporarily reinstated to haul a commemorative special train in April 1963, before finally meeting the cutter's torch in September of that year. As King (and steam) operations came to end in 1962 new diesel locomotives were introduced to take over their express train duties. The early reliability of the diesels caused some cause for concern accordingly Wolverhampton Stafford Road depot were for several weeks instructed to steam five King locos a day in order to cover for any 'modern traction' failures.

The evocative black and white steam locomotive images created by the well known photographer David Anderson accurately help to tell the story of our railways, and none more so than his comprehensive collection of GWR Castle & King images.

King class loco No 6002 KING WILLIAM IV with standard design double chimney is pictured at Didcot on 11 March 1961, No 6002 was an Old Oak Common (81A) engine at that time. Note that the distinctive King bogie design can clearly be seen and that the mechanical lubricator is positioned forward of the modified style outside steam pipe. However the mighty King carries only a Code B, ordinary stopping passenger train headlamp code. *David Anderson*

No 6002 entered GWR service in July 1927 and was first allocated to Plymouth Laira depot. BR allocations included Old Oak Common (81A) and Wolverhampton, Stafford Road (84A) from where the loco was withdrawn in September 1962.

Two interesting images of Castle class loco No 5076 GLADIATOR with a train of cattle vans. The consist is passing Foxhall Junction Didcot and taking the West curve towards Didcot North. Both images were taken as the train passed by the camera in the summer of 1961 but only on close examination was it afterwards noticed that the engine has a nameplate above the brass lined centre splasher, but it is in fact a blank with no letters on it! The loco was first named DRYSLLWYN CASTLE and renamed after a WW2 aircraft type in January 1942. In the going away shot the line which forms the North Junction can be seen beyond the bridge, ovoids are in evidence in the loco's tender and at that time the engine carried an Old Oak Common (81A) shed plate. *David Anderson.*

Loco No 5076 was originally built as DRYSLLWYN CASTLE and entered GWR service in August 1938, being first allocated to Exeter depot. Shed allocations under BR included Bristol, Bath Road (82A), Old Oak Common (81A) and Southall (81C) from where the engine was withdrawn in 1964.

Castle class loco No 5011 TINTAGEL CASTLE is pictured 'on shed' at Oxford. Points worthy of note, the loco has original valve spindle covers but BR style parallel buffer barrels. Maybe a tea break had become due? The guy clearing the smokebox has left his shovel in place among the pile of removed ash. The fireman may have to get to work with his coal pick by the look of the size of the coal lumps loaded in the Hawksworth tender, meanwhile they provide a fine landing place for the gulls! Castle locos 4073 to 5059 (and all the ex Star class rebuilds) had a rear sandbox fitted under the cab floor, with only the delivery pipe being visible. *David Anderson*

Loco No 5011 entered GWR service in July 1927 and was first allocated to Newton Abbot depot. Shed locations for this loco under BR included Newton Abbot (83A) and Old Oak Common (81A) from where the engine was withdrawn in September 1962.

Castle class No 7002 DEVIZES CASTLE is pictured at Oxford preparing to depart with an Up Worcester-Paddington train in this 1959 image, the engine would later receive a double chimney. It can be seen that the rear sandbox is fitted adjacent to the loco cab step, and thus can be externally accessed. Note also that the mechanical lubricator is in the original position behind the 'modified' pattern outside steam pipe, to facilitate access to internal motion parts the lubricators were later moved to a position forward of the steam pipe. *David Anderson.*

Loco No 7002 entered GWR service in June 1946 and was first allocated to Swansea Landore depot. Shed allocations under BR included Swansea Landore (87E) and Worcester (85A) from where the engine was withdrawn in March 1964.

King class No 6003 KING GEORGE IV is pictured at Exeter St David's station with an Up train for London Paddington on 27 July 1956. The loco is pictured here in 'wide diameter chimney' form (fitted 1954 together with a four-row superheated boiler); the engine received a standard double chimney, in July 1958. *David Anderson*

Loco No 6003 entered GWR service in July 1927 and was first allocated to Old Oak Common depot. This engine was involved in a bogie derailment incident at Midgham in August 1927 as a result of which a redesign of bogie springing on the whole of class took place. Shed allocations under BR for this loco included Old Oak Common (81A) and Cardiff Canton (88A formerly 86C) from where the loco was withdrawn in June 1962.

King class No 6019 KING HENRY V is pictured at Exeter St David's station with the same Up service on 30 July 1956, this loco received a double chimney in April 1957. Note the brazier under the water column arm on the platform end, an essential item during cold winters. *David Anderson*

Loco No 6019 entered GWR service in July 1928 and was first allocated to Wolverhampton, Stafford Road depot. BR allocations for this engine included Old Oak Common (81A) and Wolverhampton, Stafford Road (84A) from where the loco was withdrawn in September 1962.

Swindon Works, scrap line May 1962. The destruction of Castle class No 5069 ISAMBARD KINGDOM BRUNEL gets under way. Also in this picture an unidentified Hawksworth '1500' class 0-6-0 and a 'Pannier' tank await the same fate. *David Anderson*

Loco No 5069 entered GWR service in 1938 and was first allocated to Old Oak Common depot. BR allocations for this engine included Old Oak Common (81A) and Plymouth Laira (83D) from where the engine was withdrawn in February 1962.

Swindon Works. King class loco No 6011 KING JAMES I seen on the works and separated from its tender, No 6011 had only four months left in traffic when this May 1962 picture was taken. *David Anderson*

Loco No 6011 entered GWR service in April 1928 and was first allocated to Old Oak Common depot. Shed allocations under BR for this loco included Wolverhampton,

Wolverhampton Stafford Road (84A) Castle class loco No 7012 BARRY CASTLE, in very shabby exterior condition is pictured 'on shed' at Oxford in January 1965, with a Collett '6100' class 2-6-2T for company. The Castle headlamp code denotes an earlier empty stock working. *David Anderson*

Loco No 7012 entered BR service in June 1948 and was first allocated to Swansea Landore (August 1950) and March 1959 shed allocations Swansea Landore (87E); the loco was withdrawn from Wolverhampton Oxley (2B formerly 84B) in November 1964.

Castle class loco No 7013 BRISTOL CASTLE is pictured at Oxford station, note the fireman on top of the tender and the DMU in the opposite platform. It can be seen that the engine is one of several in the class which were fitted with a rather incongruous smokebox-mounted additional feed reservoir for the forward mounted mechanical lubricator. Loco No 7013 was originally No 4082 WINDSOR CASTLE see page 40. *David Anderson*